JN076202

# 敬人

## つれづれに
## 人（ひと）を敬う

【和文・英文】

5zaemon（ザエモン）
小林 利彦 著
Toshihiko Kobayashi

『敬人 つれづれに人(ひと)を敬う』を妻・順子(通称：ジュン)に捧げたい

1940年12月22日誕生・1958年4月水戸二校入学・1960年3月九段高校卒業・同年4月青短英文科入学・1962年3月卒業・1964年3月15日結婚・1964年12月26日長男：一彦誕生(日本)・1968年9月14日長女：夏子誕生(オーストラリア)・1969年9月16日次女：陽子誕生(オーストラリア)・主婦を経て2013年3月4日永眠

# Globalization
# つれづれに
# 人(ひと)を敬う

*Alexander the Great*
アレキサンダー大王

## オーストラリア国立大学総長賞授与式（1970）

オーストラリア国立大学総長兼オーストラリア中央銀行総裁ジョン・フィリップス（John Philips）と小林利彦（右）

本書は、国際商業出版株式会社『国際医薬品情報』に2018年6月～2021年4月に連載された「グローバリゼーション　つれづれに、人を敬う」を初出とし、今回の出版に際して加筆・修正を加えております。また、書名を『敬人　つれづれに人(ひと)を敬う』としました。

# はじめに、

本書は、株式会社日本医療企画の林諄代表取締役の
ご厚意により出版することができた。
謹んで感謝申し上げたい。

著者近影

雪の東京大学赤門
*The University of Tokyo Akamon in snow*

モクスワにて(1981年)

# 目次

# Contents

## 第3章 活動中の人々

## Article 3 Active the Greats ..... 85

アップジョン新講堂
開所式（1991）

Globalization
つれづれに人(ひと)を敬う

# 第1章
## アレキサンダー大王

Globalization

# Respecting People As the Time is Passing

# Article 1

## Alexander the Great

# 第1話

初出：2018年6月11日

# 人の情けが解る感性が英雄を生む

© gianmarchetti - stock.adobe.com

*Alexander the Great*
アレキサンダー大王

今、世界が必要とする透明な英雄には誰がなれるのだろうか。実在した（または）実在する人物から選んでみたい。中央政権が確立した環境でなく、自分自身が「Independent Thinker」(注)として、側近（Inner Circle）と戦略を練りに練り、実行に移して、世界を作り直した英雄は、西から東征を果たしたアレキサンダー大王（Alexander the Great、BC356年～BC323年）であり、歴史に“もし”はないが、東から西を攻める西征を計画していた日本の織田信長（Nobunaga Oda、1534年～1582年）であり、モンゴル帝国軍を完成しインドやモスクワまで支配したモンゴル平原出身のジンギス・カン（Genghis Khan、1155年～1227年）である。まあー中征とでも言おうか。もう一人、むしろ領地は減らしたが、世界を変えた男がいる。ソビエト連邦を解体したミカエル・ゴルバチョフ（Mikhail Gorbachev、1931年～）である。

まずは、アレキサンダー大王から始めたい。古代ローマの強力州であったマケドニア（Macedonia）の王であった父親フィリップ（Philip）は、13歳になった息子のアレキサンダーに家庭教師（Tutor）を付けることを決意した。選んだのは、何とアリストテレス（Aristotle、BC384年～BC322年）。理由は、学問だけでなく、両家には以前から関係があったからである。アリストテレスの父親は、マケドニア王の宮廷医だったのである。時にアリストテレス41歳である。教育は王宮ではなく田舎の

## Narrative 1

# Individuals Who Possess the Sensibility to Recognize the Benevolence of People Develop

Currently, global society needs a clear, and undisputable hero, who can this individual be? I would like to endeavor into a selection of candidates from the past and present. For instance, individuals who were within an environment of no established centralized government, who were [Independent Thinker]*, emphatically concentrated on strategies with members of their Inner Circle, such as, Alexander the Great, (BC356~BC323), on his campaign to rebuild the world from the west to conquer the east, and although history does not record 'what if', Japan's Nobunaga Oda (1534~1582) had possessed plans to advance from the east to conquer western realms. There is Genghis Khan, (1155~1227) hailing from the Mongolian plains, firmly establishes the Mongol Empire to conquer and rule lands from India to Moscow, perhaps which can be referred to as conquering the middle region. Another individual, whom ultimately decreased the land of sovereignty, but is a man who altered the world is Mikhail Gorbachev (1931~) of the Soviet Union.

I would like to begin with Alexander the Great. His father, Philip was king of the strong ancient Greek kingdom of Macedon, and when Alexander was 13 years old, his father was determined to have him placed in the care of a tutor. The tutor he selected was Aristotle, (BC384 ~ BC322). The reason behind this selection was not merely due to the academic capabilities of Aristotle, but the relationship between the two families. Aristotle's father was a physician for the royal family of Macedon. At the time of his appointment as tutor to Alexander, Aristotle was 41 years old. Education was not conducted at the palace but within a rural village, and Alexander was to be taught with a group of young men of his age. This method was taken to instill competition. Educated in this manner, just what kind of person was Alexander. Not only had he been educated in preparation for his role as a future leader, Alexander went on to study medicine, a

村で、しかも同年代の若者と共に受けたのである。競わせるのだ。その教育を受けたアレキサンダーは一体どんな人物になっていったのだろうか。先ず彼は将来のリーダーたる教育だけではなく、医学を学び後の大遠征中も生涯を通して隊員に処方・投薬を行っている。今でいう科学・技術に興味があり、遠征には動物学者・植物学者を同行させている。

頑強な身体という点では、彼自身ギリシャ神話の英雄ヘラクレス(Hercules)を生涯の目標にしていたという。

また彼は性についても禁欲主義であったといわれる。彼がまだ若かったころに、父王フィリップが妃(アレキサンダーの母親)以外の女性に子供を産ませたことを、ひどく嫌悪したことがあったからだといわれる。アレキサンダー大王が関係のあった女性は、ほんの数人である。アレキサンダー大王は、BC333年、イッソスの戦いでペルシャのダリウス3世を破った。その時ペルシャ女性のバルシネを愛人としたが、彼女は男児ヘラクレス(BC321年～BC309年)を産んでいる。その名は、前述のアレキサンダーの憧れヘラクレスから来ているのだろう。正式の結婚は、BC327年、29歳の時、相手は同じくペルシャの美女ロクサネであった。アレキサンダー大王は熱病のため急逝し、懐妊中であったロクサネは男児を出産。嫡子アレキサンダー4世であるが、アレキサンダー大王死後の混乱の中、殺害された。他の女性たちも、ヘラクレスもすべて殺されている。

話が前後するが、アレキサンダー大王はイッソスの勝利後、自らの軍人とペルシャ女性との合同結婚式を行っている。すなわち、生まれる子供はすべてギリシャ人になりギリシャの人口増加になるからであり、占領地にギリシャ人が住むことになるからである。

英雄にして、何とストイックな男なのだ！　頑強な彼の急逝はなんと考えても、残念でならない。

注)小林利彦『国際人になるためのInsight Track』第1章 第9話参照

knowledge that he utilized throughout his lifetime during long campaigns by prescribing and administering remedies to his soldiers. He was interested in what we would refer to today as science and technology, and would have zoologists and botanists accompany him in campaigns to distant lands.

Alexander's strong and muscular physique can be the result of his lifelong goal to resemble his role model, Heracles of Greek mythology.

It is also said that he was morally guarded in terms of sexuality. When Alexander was young, his father King Philip II had fathered children with women other than his mother (Olympias) which he found offensive and insulting to his mother. There are only a few women who are said to have had intimate relationships with Alexander. In BC333, in the battle of Issus where he defeated the Persian King Darius III, he met a Persian woman, Barsine who became his mistress and would later give birth to his son Heracles(BC321～BC309)naming their son after the mythological role model, he admired as noted previously. Alexander was married in BC327, when he as 29 years old, to the beautiful Persian woman, Roxana. After the sudden death of Alexander from typhoid fever, Roxana who was pregnant, gave birth to a boy. Although as heir, the boy became Alexander IV, in the turmoil that followed Alexander's death, he was assassinated. Women who were intimate with Alexander, as well as his other son Heracles, were killed.

Although not following the sequence of this narrative, after his victory at capturing Susa, he held a mass marriage ceremony of his senior officers and Persian women. In effect, children born from these unions would become Greeks, thus increasing the resident population of colonized regions with those of Greek linage.

As a hero, what a strict man! How unfortunate for such a robust man to die so suddenly.

＊) Refer to Toshihiko Kobayashi「The 10 Commandments To Become an Internationally-Minded Person」Chapter 1 Ninth Narrative

# 第2話

初出：2019年8月26日

# マケドニアの首都スコピエ(Skopje)と丹下健三(建築家)

© 朝日新聞社/アマナイメージズ

丹下健三

筆者は、スコピエ(Skopje)に来ている。スコピエの街中で、Kenzo Tangeというと“あー、あの神様か”という。1963年にスコピエを襲った大地震を思い出すからである。当時のスコピエは、チトー大統領(Josip Broz Tito)のユーゴスラビア社会主義連邦共和国(Socialist Federal Republic of Yugoslavia)の一都市であった。チトー大統領は反ソ連でむしろ資本主義に近く市民は恵まれていた。

1965年、国連がスコピエ再開発のコンペを実施した。当選したのが、当時東大教授で数々の国際建築で20世紀の建築界の寵児と言われていた丹下健三氏であった。

私にとっての丹下健三氏の建築では、東京駅近くのあの船が浮かんでいる旧東京都庁とパリを東京に持って来ちゃった新東京都庁の奇抜さである。一時期、筆者の東京の定宿がインターコンチネンタルだったこともあり、時々見上げたものである。丹下健三氏は、1987年に日本人として初めて、建築界のノーベル賞といわれるプリツカー賞(The Pritzker Architecture Prize)を受賞している。その後、槇文彦氏、安藤忠雄氏、妹島和世(Ms)氏と西沢立衛氏、そして2019年の磯崎新氏と続く。お見事！

Narrative 2

# The Capital of Macedonia Skopje and Kenzo Tange (Architect)

Within the city of Skopje, if mention is made to Kenzo Tange, "Oh, that god!" will be the reaction. It is because many of them recall the large earthquake that hit Skopje in 1963. At the time Skopje was one of the cities that made up President Josip Broz Tito's Socialist Federal Republic Yugoslavia. President Tito was anti Soviet Union, more on the side of capitalism, making the lives of its people rather enriched.

The United Nations, in 1965, held a competition focusing upon the rebuilding of Skopje. Chosen was, at the time a professor at the University of Tokyo, the international 20th Century architectural sector wonder, Kenzo Tange.

For me, the architecture of Kenzo Tange, the old Tokyo Metropolitan government structure near Tokyo station, which looks as though a ship is floating, and the originality of new Tokyo Metropolitan government building that brought Paris to Tokyo. At one time, as my regular accommodations in Tokyo was the Intercontinental, I would in some instances, take the time to look up at the structure. Kenzo Tange, in 1987 was the first Japanese to be awarded with the Pritzker Prize, the architecture world's Nobel Prize. This accomplishment was followed by Fumihiko Maki, Tadao Ando, Kazuyo Sejima(Ms.), and Ryue Nishizawa, and in 2019, Arata Isozaki. Bravo!

アレキサンダー大王が馬にまたがり槍を掲げているあの広場も、金融街の恐ろしく頑強で大きな牛の像のあたりも、市庁舎のあたりも、マケドニアのアルファベットを創設した二神像のあたりも…丹下氏の再開発の一角かと思うとカメラのシャッターも滑らかになる。100回！

丹下健三氏の後任となった香山壽夫（ひさお）教授（現名誉教授）も、不思議な縁で私と関係がある。ご尊父が東大医学部薬学科の大先輩で、第2次大戦時の満州国の総医薬務監であった。香山氏の妹君が私の妹と大学が同級生であったし、香山氏の設計による東京大学伊藤国際学術研究センターでは、良く食事をする（椿山荘カメリア）。必然のご縁である。

第4話で触れるガイドのゴッツェ・スラヴコヴスキー（Goce Slavkovski）氏に案内されて、初日の5月17日マケドニアの首都スコピエを歩くと、あぁーこれが丹下健三氏の再開発の首都かという思いであった。個人的には面識はないが、1970年代のある大みそかの午後、川崎大師で黒いオーバーを着た丹下氏ご一家に出くわしたことがある。今でもトレードマークのあの黒いオーバー姿が目に浮かぶ。

ところで首都スコピエというと、触れなくてはならない人がいる。母君がマケドニア人で首都スコピエで生まれたマザー・テレサ（Mother Teresa）である。数年前に聖人となった彼女への信頼・尊敬は大きく、影響力は強い。筆者も見学したがスコピエの最大の国立医科大学も名称をMother Teresa Medical Schoolとなったほどである。全科がそろっており、周辺国から多くの患者が来院するという。ガイドの一人シニーシャ・ナストスキー（Cinisa Nastoski）はこの病院の皮膚科の腰痛専門のセラピストだという。ちょっと休暇を取ってアルバイトだと言っていた。愉快である。夜になって、旧市街に行って骨董屋などが並ぶ街並みあたりに行ってみると、この辺りは、“あの神様ね”という声をよく聞く。坂道を登ったり下りたりと地形を生かした通りがあり、アレッ今登ったのに下りてきちゃったみたいな感じがする。丹下氏の茶目っ気ぶりが見え隠れする首都スコピエである。

The square where Alexander the Great is astride a horse wielding a spear, the surroundings of the financial district in the vicinity of a statue of a frighteningly strong bull, the government buildings, where the statues of the two divinities who founded the Macedonian alphabet, recognizing that they are a part of Mr. Tange's rebuilding outcome, I could not resist taking photos, perhaps a 100!

Professor Hisao Kohyama(currently professor emeritus), successor to Kenzo Tange, and myself have an extraordinary connection. His father, a Faculty of Pharmaceutical Sciences, University of Tokyo alumni, is a great senior of mine, during the 2nd World War, he was Manchuria's Pharmaceuticals Director General. It seems that Mr. Kayama's younger sister was classmates at university with my younger sister, and I frequently take meals(Chinzanso Camelia) located in the University of Tokyo's Itoh International Scientific Research Center, which was designed by Mr. Kayama. An inevitable relationship.

As I touched upon in my narrative 4, with my guide Goce, on the first day May 17th, as I was walking in the Macedonian capital of Skopje, ah, I thought this is the capital rebuilt by Kenzo Tange. Personally, although I have no acquaintance with him, on an afternoon of New Year's Eve in the 1970's, I ran into Mr. Tange wearing a black overcoat with his family. There are still those who do not possess a trademark. Mother Teresa, whose mother was Macedonian, was born in Skopje. Becoming a saint several years ago, trust and respect toward her is significant, her influence is strong. Leading to the largest national medical university in Skopje, be named the Mother Teresa Medical, where I also visited. Providing all courses, available and from surrounding countries a large number of patients visit this medical institution. One of the guides, Sinisa is a therapist for a lower back pain specialist of the dermatology department. Saying that he was taking a little time off to do some part time work. Quite delightful. Evening comes, and when I visit the old town where the streets are lined with antique shops, it is in the area that I hear a voice saying "That god". A slope way utilizing the formation of the land, that makes one climb up and down, wait a minute, I thought I just climbed up, now I feel as though I am going down. The playfulness of Mr. Tange appears and disappears in the capital of Skopje.

## 第3話

初出：2019年10月28日

# マケドニア・イスタンブール アラカルト(a la carte)

*Alexander the Great*
アレキサンダー大王

2019年5月18日(土曜日)、ホテル・DoubleTree by Hiltonに着くや否や、フロントのマーチン・デンコフスキー(Martin Denkovski)氏から、いきなりイギリス英語　で"I am keeping an Akita－inu(秋田犬／アキタイヌ)"と話しかけられビックリ。名刺には秋田犬と自分の写真入りと来りゃー、イヌ・クレイジー(crazy)も本物でござんす！

それをさかのぼること2日前の5月16日、三極用のアダプターをイスタンブール(Istanbul)のホテル・エリート・ワールド(Elite World)のフロントで尋ねると50USドルで売るという、借りたいというと貸すことはできないルールである。スーパーに行けば売っている､13USドル位という。仕方がない。タクシーで行ってイスタンブールのスーパーマーケットで三極用のアダプターを買おうとしていると、立派な貴婦人がお手伝いしましょうと滑らかな英語で話しかけてくれ、確かに13USドル位で買うことができました。折角だから、目の前のスターバックスでコーヒーをと誘ったら、OKと頷いてスターバックスへ。小一時間､日本特に沖縄のことをおしゃべりし、お金を払おうとしたら、入るときにもう払ったという。それは…という

Narrative 3

# Macedonia・Istanbul a la Carte

*Brick Building (right top) was Alexander-born-place*

Starting with, Saturday, May 18th Hotel: DoubleTree by Hilton, I had barely arrived at the front desk, when the attendant, Martin Denkovski, immediately started talking in English, "I am keeping an Akita-inu (Akita breed dog), taking by surprise. Including a photograph of his Akita-inu alongside himself on his business card, well, it reflects his affection for the dog borders on 'dog crazy'.

Going back 2 days: May 16th, I found that I would need a three-prong adapter. When I went to the front desk of the hotel; Elite World, Istanbul, I was told that it would cost 50 U.S. dollars, where upon I conveyed that I would just like to borrow the adapter, I was told that it was against their rules, and I would have to purchase it. I was told that the same item is sold at a local supermarket for about 13 U.S. dollars. Well, there was nothing left to do. So, I took a taxi to the local supermarket to buy a three-prongs adapter, where I was approached by a handsome lady who kindly offered her assistance in fluent English, leading to the successful purchase of the item at 13 U.S. dollars. In return for her kindness, as there was a Starbucks located right in front of us, I invited her to a cup of coffee, which she accepted. For a little over an hour, we talked, mainly about Okinawa and Japan, I was about to pay for the coffee, when she told me

と、昨年訪ねた沖縄で大変な“おもてなし”を受けたお礼だという。

ありがとうございましたで、タクシーで帰る。タクシー代合わせて60USドルなにがし。ハハーン、フロントが言った謎が解けました…。でも、スーパーも見たし、おもてなしのトルコの貴婦人にもお会いできたし、コリャー、来る早々縁起がイーワイ！　マケドニアが楽しみ！

5月17日朝、ホテル(DoubleTree by Hilton)にガイドのゴッツェ・スラヴコヴスキー(Goce Slavkovski)とドライバーのシニーシャ・ナストスキー(Cinisa Nastoski)が来てくれ、4日間の日程調整をして車(Mercedes)に乗るといきなり“Alexander is a gay！(アレキサンダーはゲイだ！)という。いきなりでビックリ！　まあー、アレキサンダーもロクサネ(Roxane)というペルシャの美人妻も居たし、考えてみると時代は違っても、日本の戦国時代でも小姓は居たし、戦場ではそんなもんか。マケドニアの車は、ほぼメルセデス・ベンツである。旅行中見た日本車は一台のパジェロだけであった。

ところで、マケドニアで急逝した大王の遺体をどのようにして首都ペラ(Pella in Greece)に移したのだろうか。ミイラ化して麻布でしっかりと包んで移送したということであった。そして誕生の首都ペラに奥深く墓を作り埋葬されたという。そこまで歩いて行ったが、観光資源として一般公開の整備中で見ること能わず。拝むのみ、合掌。その遺体は、盗掘に遭い、今どこにあるのかは不明とのことであった。

後述になるが、ファイナンシャル・タイムズ(Financial Times)が大英博物館でこの夏8月にアレキサンダー大王の特別展覧会を計画していると伝え、彼の世によく知られている大理石像(少し鼻が欠けている)の写真がFT週刊誌(5月10日の週)に載っていた。その顔は何とも寂しく今にも涙がこぼれそうである。多分､彼は自らの急逝をなんとも無念・残念に思ったのであろう。あるいは、この大理石像を彫った彫刻家が大王の急逝を無念に思い、その想いが大王の顔に表れたのであろうか。

that she had paid for it when we entered. Wait, this is not what I intended, that is when she said that when visiting Okinawa last year, she received such great 'hospitality' that she wanted me to consider it as an expression of gratitude.

Well, thank you very much, and I took a taxi to the hotel. Including the taxi fare the total came to roughly 60 U.S. dollars. Okay, I solved the mystery behind what the front desk initially said. But all was not lost, I was able to see the supermarket, encountered a lovely Turkish lady of great hospitality, it is a good start indeed! I look forward to Macedonia!

The morning of May 17th, the guide Goce Slavkovski and driver Cinisa Nastoski arrived at the hotel DoubleTree by Hilton, and after we coordinated the 4-day schedule, when we piled into the car (Mercedes) to start our journey, suddenly "Alexander is gay!" was pronounced. It was so sudden that I was surprised! Alexander had a beautiful Persian wife Roxane, but come to think of it, although the period is different, during Japan's Warring States, there was the existence of pageboys, on battlefields they were probably necessities. In Macedonia the majority of cars were Mercedes Benz. The one Japanese automobile I came across was a Pajero.

By the way, the body of the great king (Alexander), who passed away suddenly in Macedonia was likely to have been taken to the capital Pella in Greece. It is said that his body was mummified and tightly wrapped in hemp cloth to be transported. Laid to rest in the place of his birth, the capital Pella, where a tomb was prepared deep within the ground. Walking to the sight, being under preparation as a tourist site for the general public, unfortunately, I was not allowed in. I could only offer my prayers by placing my hands together. Grave robbers have dug up this sight, which have resulting in the loss of his remains.

Although described later, according to an article in the Financial Times, the British Museum was planning a special exhibit o Alexander the Great this summer in August, a photograph of the well-known marble head (nose slightly chipped) of Alexander was in the weekly edition of the Financial Times (week of May 10th). The expression captured on this bust is one of loneliness, almost as though he is about to shed a tear. It can be assumed that he was lamenting and regretting his sudden death. Or, it may be that the sculptor who had made this marble bust was lamenting and regretting the sudden death of the great king, which was reflected upon the features of the great king.

# 第4話

初出：2019年6月24日

# アレキサンダー大王の国マケドニア
# ——人々とその素顔

シニーシャ(理学療法士)、小生、自宅提供者、警官、ゴッツェ(案内人・大学院生)

トルコ最大の会議斡旋会社・ALPHA社のセールス代表のシナン・セネム(Sinan Senem)を通してマケドニア観光局が斡旋してくれたガイドであるゴッツェ・スラヴコヴスキー(Goce Slavkovski)とシニーシャ・ナフトスキー(Cinisa Nastoski)によると、アレキサンダー大王よりも父親のフィリップ2世大王(Philip 2nd Great)の方が評価が高いのである。アレキサンダー大王は、その有り余る才能で、全てを自分で取り仕切ったのは良いのだが、息子も大きくなる前に、また後継者も決めないうちに早逝したのが運が悪かったと言うのである。父親(フィリップ2世大王)はアレキサンダー大王のような立派な後継者をタイミングよく育てたではないかと言う。そう言われるとなるほどそうかとも思う。アレキサンダー大王が早逝したのがまずかったと言うのだが、なぜ早逝したのかは次の第5話で触れたいと思う。

ここで、少しマケドニア(北マケドニア共和国)の文化と人々について触れたいと思う。まず、人口(約200万人)の約7割が正統派キリスト教徒(Orthodox Christians)であり、残りがイスラム教徒と他の宗教であ

Narrative 4

# Alexander the Great's Nation Macedonia —— The People, Their Feature

マケドニアの「料理の鉄人(右端)」

It was Sinan Senem, who is a sales representative for ALPHA, which is Turkey's largest arrangement firm, coordinated with Macedonia's Tourism Organization which arranged two guides; Goce Slavkovski and Cinisa Nastoski, shared that Alexander's father, Philip II, has higher reputation than Alexander himself. Although Alexander the Great, possessing unlimited capability, and he had totally controlled every aspect, his misfortunate was in that he passed away before his son was of age, and not determining a successor. When told that his father, Phillip II, had raised an outstanding successor such as Alexander the Great, upon hearing this, I have to say that I would agree. His father, Philip II is Alexander Big. Reference to the misfortune of Alexander the Great's yearly death is made, I would like to touch upon why this occurred in the next narrative 5.

Let us take a brief look at the people and culture of Macedonia (North Republic of Macedonia). To start with, 70% of the population (roughly 2 million), are Orthodox Christians, the remaining are Muslim and other religions. They are all friendly and polite. The spirit of 'O-Mo-Te-Nashi', or hospitality is thoroughly present.

るという。皆、親切で丁寧である。“おもてなし”／O-Mo-Te-Nashiの心が、行き届いているのだ。

困ったことは、男性はほぼ煙草（シガレット）を吸っている。パッケージを見ると“煙草はあなたを殺します”と書いてある。ちゃんと書いてあるじゃないかと言うと、「マケドニアの空気が良過ぎるので、肺のバランスを取っているのさ」と来る。将にブラックユーモアで、人々は明るい。

ところで、2人のガイドの姓からお気付きかもしれないが、姓の末尾が…スキー（…ski）となっている。第二次世界大戦後、全国民の姓の末尾がスキー（…ski）となったのだとか。これは、ロシアをはじめスラブ系の影響を強く受けているからだという。全国民が一つの大家族と考えているのだろう。結果、同姓同名がたくさんいるという。しかし、同姓同名であることに興味はなく、一緒に何かをするという考えはなく、個人は自由に行動している。

また世界の中心はマケドニアであると信じている節がある。さすがアレキサンダー大王の国。ガイドの条件に、夕食とガソリン代は筆者持ちになっていたので、レストランは一流どころを選び、マケドニアのラム（Lamb）、マケドニアの野生狩猟肉（Hunting meats）に彼らも筆者もご満悦。ガソリン代を支払ったので、1リットルの計算から、マケドニアのデナールは、日本円に比して5分の1位であることも分かった。そうするとガイド料金も彼らにとってはごっつぁんだったことになる。とにかく頑張ってくれたのも分かる気がするし、ありがたかった。また、マケドニアは数値はデジタル化しており、目方はグラムで距離はキロである。数値の世界的統一をにらんでの先取りである。ただ、米国（マイル、ガロン）と英国（マイル／キロ、ポンド）が変わるかどうかであるが…。

前述したが、人々は親切で丁寧である。ビジネスマンは身だしなみ着こなし抜群で、ほぼ全員がヒゲを生やしており、よく似合っている。女性はマケドニア風の美人が多く、ビジネスにも進出しているが眼鏡をかけている方が多い。しかも黒縁眼鏡で、顔が引き締まって見え、恰好がよい。

The problem was most all men were smoking cigarettes. On the packages the phrase "Smoking Kills" is written. When I point out that its clearly written, they come back with "Macedonia's air is too clean, so we are balancing our lungs". Precisely, black humor, the people are cheerful and spirited.

By the way, perhaps there may be those of you who have noticed that the last names of my two guides end with (. . . ski). Following the end of World War II, I was told that the entire public added (. . .ski) to their last names. According to the explanation, it is through the strong influence beginning with Russian and the Slavs. Perhaps they thought of the entire public as one large family. I was told that this resulted in a significant number of people having the same first and last name. However, there is no interest in whether they share the same last and first names, or of thinking of what can be done together, individuals freely go about their business.

There is a perception that Macedonia is the center of the world. Perhaps a profound legacy of Alexander the Great. The guides terms were that dinner and gasoline was to be paid by me, their choice of restaurants was the best; feasting on Macedonia lamb, and hunting meats, the gentlemen and myself were extremely satisfied. Since I paid for the gasoline, when calculating from 1 liter, Macedonia's denar rate compared to the Japanese yen, I found that it was probably one fifth. From this, I can easily assume the guide fee that these gentlemen received was a nice pay day, thus the efforts they showed is understandable, which I am grateful for. In addition, Macedonia's numerals have been digitalized, and weights are in grams, distances are reflected in kilos. They have advanced early in adapting the global unification. But, whether the U.S.'s (mile, gallon) and the U.K.'s (mile/kilo, pound) will change is another matter.

As I noted earlier, the people are kind and polite. Businessmen are well dressed and wear their attire with noticeable style, the majority sport beards, which are very becoming. Most of the women are Macedonian beauties, advancing into the business sector, I noted that a large number wore glasses. Black framed glasses were the norm, enhancing a sharpness to the face, very attractive.

## 第5話

初出：2019年8月12日

# アレキサンダー大王——異母弟プトレマイオスと忠臣プトレマイオス

© Science Photo Library/amanaimages

忠臣プトレマイオス

アレキサンダー大王(BC356年〜BC323年)の東征の地図を見ると気が遠くなるような感じがする。なぜアレキサンダー大王の軍隊は強かったのか。父フィリップ2世大王は、歩兵を1万人から2万4千人に増加、騎兵隊を600人から3500人に増加して速攻性を高めた。また槍は長くし、盾は頑丈にして装備の改革。もはや民兵ではなく、軍人・軍隊となったのである。それを息子のアレキサンダー大王は引き継ぎ、連戦連勝を重ねることになる。

まず、アレキサンダー大王は、広大な王宮殿ペラを出発して今のトルコ・アンカラのグラニコス(Granicus)で初戦を難なく突破し、次いでイッソス(Issus)で精鋭部隊を率いるダリウス3世(Darius 3rd、BC380年〜BC330年)と対峙(BC333年)、負け戦だったといわれる劣勢をひっくり返し勝利を収めた。ここでアレキサンダー大王の大王たる地位が確立する。ダレイオス3世は、名君といわれる人物だったようであるが、時に49歳。何しろ血気盛んな25歳のアレキサンダーには気力でも及ばなかったのだろう。

こうして先進国ペルシャのマケドニア・ギリシャ化に成功し、ペルシャ貴族の息女ロクサネ(Roxane、16歳)と結婚し(BC327年)、彼女はアレキサンダー大王の最初の妃となった。大王はBC326年の東方遠征にロクサネを帯同している。

# Alexander the Great —— Half-Brother Philip III Arrihidaeus and Loyal Retainer Ptolemy

© Yaroslav - stock.adobe.com

Looking at the map of Alexander the Great's (BC356 ~ 323) eastern expedition, is mind boggling. What was behind the strength of Alexander the Great's army? His father, Philip II increased the number of his foot soldiers from 10,000 to 24,000 and his calvary from 600 to 3,500, heightening its characteristics in speed. There were also reforming measures taken toward the equipment of combat, such as; increasing the length of spears, and strengthening shields. They were was no longer a militia group, but became trained soldiers and an organized army. This army was inherited by Alexander the Great who utilized it to successfully win battle after battle.

Alexander the Great departed from the enormous palace in Pella to Granicus, which is what is now known as Ankara, Turkey, to engage in his first battle, which he won with ease, followed by the Battle of Issus in which Darius III (BC380 ~ 330) took personal command of his elite army, and what was predicted initially as a battle that would that would end in defeat, Alexander managed to turn the tide, becoming victorious. This is the point in which Alexander the Great establishes his position as a great king. Darius III, although he was known as an exceptional king, at the time he was 49 years old. It is extremely likely that, he could not compete with the vitality and willpower of the 25-year-old Alexander.

Successfully turning the advanced nation of Persia and Macedonia to become a Greek, which lead to the wedding(BC327)between Alexander the Great and the no-

さて、アレキサンダー大王は壮大な東征を果たし、インドからの帰途、バビロン（Babylon）でインドで罹患したマラリア（Malaria）で約1カ月の療養で急逝したといわれている。何故あの頑強な世界を制覇した男がマラリアなどで命を落とすのか。考えられない！　わたくしは、異母弟プトレマイオス3世フィリップが関係していると邪推している。当時の薬は煎じ薬であり、毒草も数多とあった。この異母弟には、アレキサンダー大王の母君オリンピアも大変警戒をしていた。可愛くて可愛くて仕方なかった母オリンピアにとっては、この急逝は何たる悲劇であったであろうか。怖いもの無しの大王が、ただ一人怖かったというのが教育ママのオリンピアであったという。

大王の急逝後合議制が組織され、幸いロクサネは懐妊中でありその出産を待って次の大王を決めることになった。ロクサネは男児を出産し、アレキサンダー4世となりアレキサンダー大王の正式な後継者となった。しかし、ゼロ歳。数名による摂政が敷かれた。その一人カッサンドロス（Kassandros）が後継者になろうとして反乱を起こし、ロクサネ他を殺戮した。

アレキサンダー大王は、もともとエジプトのアレキサンドリアにマケドニア・ギリシャ王朝を築こうと考えていた。アリストテレス教室の学友であり無二の親友でもあったストール・プトレマイオスをエジプトに駐留させていた。摂政の一人でもあった彼がカッサンドロスの反乱後直ちにマケドニアに引き返し、これを鎮圧。新たにアレキサンダー大王の後継としてのプトレマイオス王朝を創設し、クレオパトラの死まで続いたのである（BC305年～BC30年）。鼻が高くて有名な彼女はマケドニア・ギリシャ人であったが、アレキサンダー大王の直系ではない。当時エジプトに残っていたユダヤの奴隷たちは、大王によるエジプト開放により、身分を解かれ市民権を得た。そして、大王を救済の神（メシア）として尊敬したという。

ble woman Roxane (16 years old), she was Alexander the Great's first wife. He takes her along in his expedition to the east of BC326.

Alexander the Great, accomplishing his eastern expedition, was making his return home from India, infected with malaria in India, it is said that he passed away in Babylon where he was being treated for approximately one month. How could a man who conquered such a tough world lose his life to malaria? Hard to imagine! I have a groundless suspicion that his half-brother Philip III Arrhidaeus was involved. At the time medicine was in the form of herbal decoction, poisonous herbs were abundant, and Alexander the Great's mother Olympias was extremely cautious. Olympias adored him; his sudden death was understandably a huge tragedy to her. The fearless great king, perhaps the one person he was frighten of was his education-minded mother Olympias.

Following the sudden death of the great king, a council system was established, fortunately, Roxane was pregnant, a decision was made to await the birth of the child before proclaiming the next king. Roxane gave birth to a boy, who became Alexander IV and official successor to Alexander the Great. However, not yet a year old. There were a number of guardians in a newly established regency. One of them was Kassandros, looking to be the successor to the empire, started a rebellion in which Roxane, among others were murdered.

Originally, Alexander the Great, had intended to establish a Greek Hellenistic empire in Egypt's Alexandria. A classmate of Aristotle tutorial classroom and singularly close friend, Ptolemy Soter was stationed in Egypt by Alexander. As one of the guardians of the regency, upon learning of the rebellion by Kassandros, he immediately returned to Macedonia to suppress it. As the new successor to Alexander the Great, he established the Ptolemaic dynasty (BC305 ~ 30) which continued until the death of Cleopatra. Famously known for the height of her nose, although she was a Macedonian Greek, she is not a direct descendant of Alexander the Great. The Jewish slaves who remained in Egypt during this period, were released from bondage by the great king, receiving citizenship. Leading to the great king to be respected as a savior god (messiah).

## 第6話

初出：2019年9月9日

# アレキサンダー大王と父フィリップ2世大王

*King Philip II*
フィリップ2世大王
© Science Photo Library/amanaimages

BC5世紀～BC4世紀ころのマケドニアを含むギリシャは後進国で、ペルシャが先進国であった。フィリップ2世大王の築いたバルカン王国ですら調度品、食事作法までダリウス3世で有名なペルシャ式であった。この先進国にチャレンジしたのが、父フィリップ2世大王とアレキサンダー大王なのだ。ペルシャ式をギリシャ風に変える。

さて、父フィリップ2世大王は、マケドニアならずギリシャを含み、一部ルーマニアを含むバルカン大帝国を築き上げた。したがって当時の首都は、現在のスコピエ(Skopje)でなく、ギリシャのペラ(Pella)にあった。

5月22日朝7時に出発した我々は、途中軽食を取り時速120キロで車を飛ばして、マケドニアを出国しギリシャに入国しペラに着いたのは午後2時であった。王宮殿のあったペラは見渡す限りの広さで、奈良の平城京とは比較にならず、車は許されず歩くほかはなく、歩くこと数時間でヤッとアレキサンダー大王の眠る墓までたどり着いた。ちょうど大王の洞窟の奥深い墓を一般公開し観光に役立てようという趣旨で改装中で中に入れず、手を合わせるのみ。そこからギリシャを出国しマケドニア

## Narrative 6

# Alexander the Great and His Father, the Great King Philip II

In the time of BC5~4 Greek, including Macedonia were undeveloped countries, Persia was a developed nation. Within the Balkan kingdom established by Philip II, furniture and the manner of meals were that of the famous Persian style of King Darius III. Challenging this developed nation was father Philip II the Great and Alexander the Great. Altering the Persian style into Greek style.

Philip II the Great's established a Balkan empire that included not only Macedonia but Greece and a portion of Rumania. Thus, the capital was not located in the current Skopje, but in Greece's Pella.

Departing at 7 in the morning of May 22, and taking a light meal along the way, our car was traveling at a speed of 120 kilos and hour, leaving the boarders of Macedonia and entering Greece arriving at Pella at 2 in the afternoon. The remains of the royal palace of Pella was an expanse as far as the eye could see, far larger in comparison to Nara's Heijyokyo, since cars are not allowed, all is left is to walk, the walk took several hours to finally reach the grave in which Alexander the Great sleeps. It just so happened that the grave, located deep within the great king's cave, was under renovations in preparation for public viewing to assist in promoting tourism, I could only put my hands together in respect. Departing Greece from there to enter Macedonia, repeating passport checks, it was straight to a restaurant. The establishment specializes in hunting meat (gibier in French, gibbier in English), a delicious meal of fresh venison prepared in the Macedonian style. Delightfully full. When I returned to the hotel it was after 9 at night.

Returning to the father, Philip II. I visited his grave the day before on May 21, it was a deep cave grave carved from hard rock, it was extremely large and dignified. This father king's grave is located in Macedonia, because he was assassinated in this region. He didn't smoke, nor drink, listening to the voices of his subjects he governed them with goodness, and was loved by his soldiers. When in combat, he won every battle. When it came to the education of his son Alexander, he reflected his excellence in

に入国とパスポートチェックを繰り返し、レストランへまっしぐら。ハンチング・ミートのジビエ(仏：gibier、英：gibbier)の店で、捕りたての鹿肉のマケドニア風料理で舌鼓。満腹でうっとり。ホテルに戻ったのは、21時過ぎ。

さて父フィリップ2世大王に話を戻したい。彼のお墓を前日、5月21日に訪ねたが、その洞窟墓は奥深く岩石つくりの凄く広い威厳のあるものであった。この父王の墓がマケドニアにあるのは、彼がこの地で暗殺されたからである。彼は、たばこもやらず、酒もやらず、民の声を聴く善政を施し、民からも、将軍たちからも、そして兵からも慕われていた。戦えば、連戦連勝。そして息子アレキサンダーを教育するのに、ソクラテスの一番弟子アリストテレスを家庭教師に選んだのは秀逸。いかにマケドニアの将来を考えていたのかが分かる。

しかし、この選択には二つの仕掛けがあったとみている。一つは征服した城主から息子と同年配の息子達約20人を選択し教育をする。ペルシャ式だった生活様式の代わりにギリシャ風を教え込む。いずれペルシャ風を改めるよう、いずれペルシャを征服するのだからと、洗脳する。もう一つは、この息子たちを人質としても扱う。お見事！

日本の戦国時代と同じである。やっと、マケドニア・ギリシャの戦国時代が統一されようとしていたのである、フィリップ2世大王によって。

ところが伏兵がいたのだ。好事魔多し、日本の戦国時代と同じくマケドニアでも王には小姓(loverと呼んでいた)がおり、一番の小姓であったパウサニアス(Pausanias)は、新たに採用された小姓に嫉妬し、大王自らの娘クレオパトラ(アレキサンダーの実妹でもある)と王妃オリンポスの甥との結婚式祝宴の最中に、こともあろうにフィリップ2世大王をひと突きにして殺害したのである。まことにあっけないフィリップ2世大王の終焉。この大混乱を収拾したのは、アレキサンダー大王(BC356年～BC323年)である。時にBC336年、20歳の若武者である。同じく若武者の源義経を彷彿とさせられた。

choosing Aristotle; the best pupil of Socrates, as his tutor. It is easy to understand how he was thinking of the future of Macedonia.

However, I think that this choice had two catches to it. One was to have roughly 20 chosen boys, of the same age as his son who were sons of rulers that he had conquered to be educated. This was to instruct the Greek lifestyle in place of what was Persian. In time change the Persian ways, in time we are going to conquer Persia, brainwashing. The other was to, in essence utilize these boys as hostages. Brilliant!

It is the same as Japan's Warring States Period. Finally, the warring state period of Macedonia and Greece was going to unification by Philip II the Great.

However, there was an ambush. Happy events have many evils, as the same in Japan's Warring State period, Macedonia's king also had a lover, his favorite was Pausanias, becoming jealous of a new lover, during the wedding celebrations of the king's own daughter, Cleopatra (Alexander's sister), to the queen Olympias's nephew, to stab him to death. A rather disappointing death of Philip II the Great. Ending this great disturbance was Alexander the Great (BC356 ~ 323). The year was BC336, the young warrior was 20 years old. Reminiscent of another young warrior, Minamoto no Yoshitsune.

フィリップ2世(BC382年～BC336年)の暗殺公開

Globalization
つれづれに人(ひと)を敬う

# 第2章

## 過ぎし日の方々

Globalization

# Respecting People As the Time is Passing

# Article 2

## Passing the Greats

## 第 7 話

初出：2021年4月12日

# 産官学の申し子――Ted Cooper

THE UPJOHN COMPANY

T. COOPER, M.D.
Chairman of the Board and
Chief Executive Officer
TELEPHONE: (616) 323-7094

March 23, 1993

Dr. Toshihiko Kobayashi
Upjohn Pharmaceuticals Limited
Tsukuba Research Laboratories
23 Wadai, Tsukuba City
Ibaraki Pref 300-42
Japan

Dear Toshi:

Now that I am back at work part time, I wanted to thank you not only for your note, but for the good luck charm from the Tsukuba shrine -- it's working and I am feeling quite well. One of these days I will get back to Japan.

Thanks again for support and thoughtfulness.

Best regards,

Ted

Theodore Cooper

*Ted Cooper*
テッド・クーパー

このTedのサインは、意識が朦朧とする中、息を引き取る直前に書かれたという。ひょっとしたらTedは、それまでの上司とスタッフという関係からだけでなく、僕を息子と思って可愛がってくれていたのかという気がする。

Ted Cooper MD,Ph.D.（Ted）の曽祖父は、最後のロシア皇帝ニコライ2世の20世紀初頭のポツロム（異邦人追放）でロシアを追放され、米国に移住したユダヤ人の家系である。ニューヨークのブルックリンでビールの配達業（Pabst社）をしていた。Tedは、一念発起MD,Ph.D.となった。

若い頃のTedは、土曜日にはシナゴークに行き、日曜日もキリスト教会の周りをウロウロしていた。ターゲットは、教会でなく聖歌隊の歌姫の一人だった。それがオシドリ夫婦となったパテー（Patey、通称ヴィヴィアン／Vivian、ご家族がフランス出身）であった。

*Willian U Parfet*

二人は、男の子人と女の子2人の4人の子宝に恵まれ

## Narrative 7

# Ted Cooper

## ——A prototype of Industry–Authority–Academia

*Jerry Mitchell*

*Tim Gumbleton*

*Jeremy Wentworth*

*Doug Morton*

*Tim Franson*

Ted Cooper's signature "Ted"on his letter attached hereon on was done by himself just before coma ,then he had come to coma leading to his untimely demise.I am feeling that more than the relationship as CEO and Board Chairman ,he may had treated me , as if I was his son.

Ted Cooper MD,PhD's(Ted) great-grand father was a Jewish ousted from Russia at the beginning of the 20th century/so called "Potulom／ポツロム" ,and moved to the US. In Manhattan-Brocklin in New York city as a beer-carrier business(Pabst Company).

Ted in young used to synagogue on Saturday, and further on Sunday, he walked around Church close to the above synagogue ,he aimed to visit the church,but his objective is not the church ,his target was a beautiful and wonderful lady,being a beautiful singer of Singer Group of the church,who was his current wife (Patty) ever-since .

They had been gifted by two(2) children. One of them was a son who was Director of Upjohn-Cafeteria ,and the second was a father-resembling daughter who became a lawyer in WDC.

The Upjohn Founder ,Dr.Upjohn also in short used to have talked with Ted in the same eye-eye in face to face.One of Ted's specific treatment on me was I am short just like Ted.Also Armitage ,Head of Upjohn-Properties was short who was promoted by Ted up to Secretary of US Patent Office. Short-Short ! Relevant to this phenomena,an interesting black humor was ,Ted drove his father's Beer-Carrier-Car to Upjohn Head Office,enjoying watching staff-cars down. The Empty Upjohn CEO-Car was following ....

た。奥様のパテーとは33年の結婚生活で、いつもボスはパテーだと自認していた。とにかく超多忙だったから。創業家のアップジョン氏(Dr. Upjohn)とは、「eye to eye」で話をした。二人とも小柄だったから。筆者も小柄だったし、UpjohnからUS特許庁長官になったArmitageも小柄で、ともにTedには可愛がってもらった。面白い逸話がある。Tedは通勤に公用車を使わず親父(おやじ)が使っていたビール配達用トラックで通勤していた。この時くらいは、「上から目線」を楽しんでいたのだろうという冗談が…。

とにかく、Tedはいつもニコニコしているが、ひとたび激怒すると周りが震え上がった。筆者は、用事があるときは前日予約を入れ、早朝7時にオフィスを訪ねていた。ある朝、Tedのガンガン怒鳴る声がして、そっと覗いて見ると、FDAコミッショナー代行を務め当時アップジョンの出頭副社長(No. 2 in Upjohn)だったMark Novitch(M.N.)氏が額に手を当てうなだれて聞いているではないか。7時になり筆者がオフィスに入り、解放。しかし、Tedの1993年4月24日の訃報(64歳、骨髄腫)とともにM.N.氏も退任した。

さて、Tedの「産官学の申し子」の本質に迫りたい。“学”としては、母校のジョンズホプキンス大学医学部(専門は心臓外科)の医学部長として大学の運営に能力を発揮した。そして、“官”としては厚生・教育省長官であったワインバーガー(Weinberger)氏の厚生教育次官補として、ワインバーガー氏が後にペンタゴン(国防総省)の長官となった時、Tedは国防長官補佐にさらなる栄進をした。そして“産”としてはファミリー以外で初めてのアップジョンCEOを歴任したのを見れば、「産官学の申し子」は一目瞭然である。

また直属の上司だったジェリー・ミッチェル(Dr.J.Michel)。就任の日にカウボーイの衣装で現れたテキサス男。何故か、気が合うて忘られぬ。

Anyhow, Ted used to be smiling .But,once he burst into furious ,everybody came to be trembled under rattling !! When I had a business with him ,I usually get his appointment at 7AM in Executive Office Building ,so called Targe Mahal in Upjohn ,being all over glassy. Once I arrived there at 6:30 AM,Ted was shouting against Mark Novitch who was then-No2 following Ted in Upjohn,and had been an Associate Commissioner in FDA was of a face down with his elbow on front of his head,and listening to Ted. At 7 AM, I knocked door, then he was relieved .The reason was that Minoxidil /hair growth was not listed in pricing by FDA.

Anyhow, Ted as a charismatic prototype of Industries-Authority-Academia was clearly shown by the above.

Also ,my direct boss:, Dr. Jerry Mitchell as a typical Texan. He , the day when joined Upjohn ,wore a cowboy hat as well as cowboy costume upsetting all executives including Ted . Frankly,that was not Ted's style. But neither matter. Both of us feeling well ,and never forgettable. Even after retirement ,we are still communicating as friends.

*Lawyer Keishi Komoriya*
籠屋恵嗣弁護士

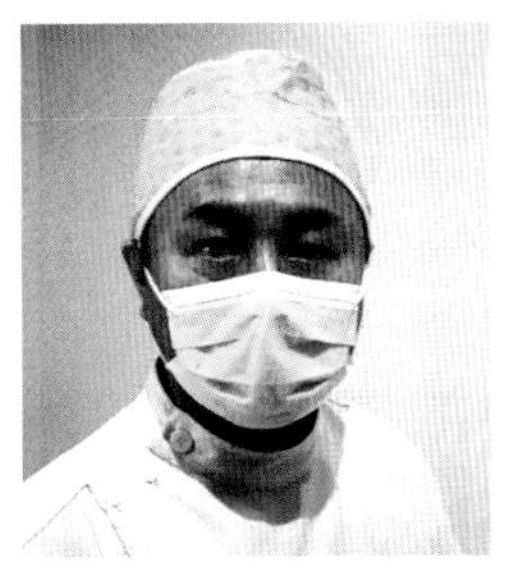

*Toshio Asaumi*
浅海登志雄
（浅海歯科医院 理事長）

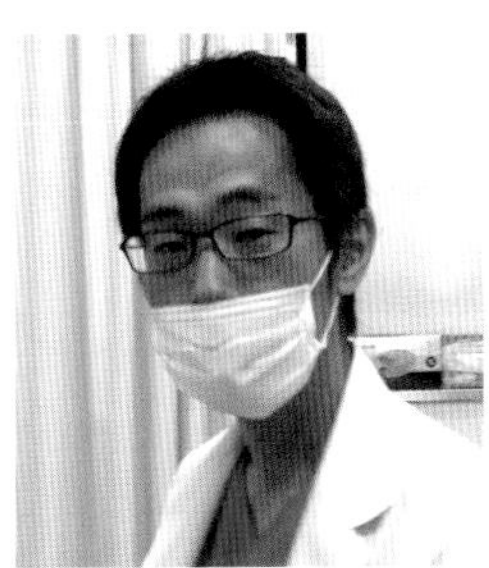

*Takeshi Hamada*
濱田　毅（東大医学部附属病院消化器内科専門医 准教授）

*Lawyer Koichi Yonekawa*
米川耕一弁護士

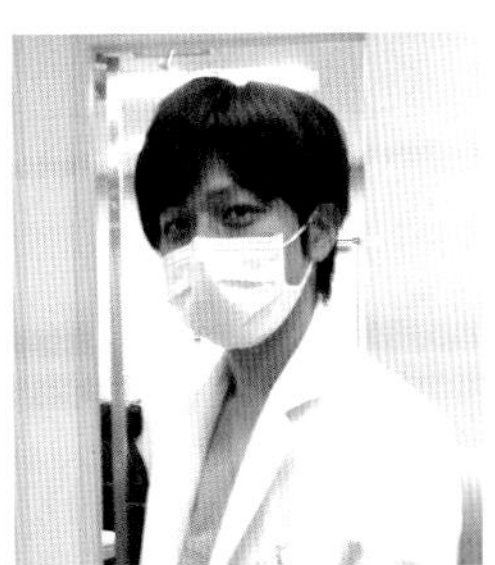

*Hiroya Mizutani*
水谷浩哉（東大医学部附属病院消化器内科 特任臨床医）

## 第8話

初出：2018年7月9日

# 二人の神様、今や静——物(もの)から動——物(もの)へ

*Konosuke Matsushita*
松下幸之助

© 朝日新聞社／アマナイメージズ

二人の神様とは、ジョン・フランシス・"ジャック"・ウェルチ・ジュニア(John Francis "Jack" Welch Jr.)と松下幸之助氏である。

ご承知のごとく、松下電気器具製作所(現パナソニック)の創業者である松下幸之助翁(1894年〜1989年)は「お客様は神様です」と言ったといわれているが、本当にそう感じていたのであろう。父親の事業失敗で、丁稚奉公するなかで学んだ「一人勝ちは良くない」という自覚が、時を経て翁身らを商売の神様と周囲の人々を言わしめたのである。

一方、General Electricの元会長兼CEOのジャック・ウェルチ氏(1935年〜2020年)は、アイルランド系の米国人である。カトリック教徒である。ここで二人の神様に大きな違いが窺える。ウェルチ氏は、松下翁と違って創業者ではない。これは、両人の年齢差がほぼ40年(松下翁が年長)と無関係ではないであろう。米国では、英国の産業革命の波が来ていたであろうから。勿論、パナソニックやGEの歴史・現実を語るつもりなど毛頭ない。ただ面白いことに両雄の次世代にそれぞれジェフ・

## Narrative 8

# Two Gods,The Current Shift from Stationary Items to Items of Motion

© ZUMA Press/amanaimages

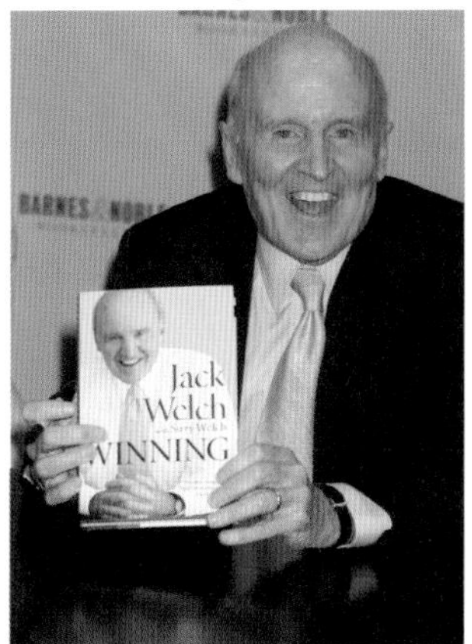


*John Francis "Jack" Welch Jr.*
"ジャック"・ウェルチ・ジュニア氏

The 'Two Gods' that I referred to here are John Francis 'Jack' Welch Jr. and Konosuke Matsushita.

As many may be aware, Konosuke Matsushita (1894~1989)is the founder of Matsushita Electric Houseware Manufacturing Works (present-day Panasonic), who is said to have often say 'Customers are our Gods', however did he really have this perception. After the failure of his father's enterprise, he went into apprentice service where he learned 'winning alone is unfavorable' an awareness which as time passed led to reference to Matsushita as 'the God of Business' from those surrounding him.

On the other hand, former Chairman and CEO of General Electric, Jack Welch(1935~) is an American of Irish decent, and Catholic. Here I will point out the significant difference between these two 'Gods'. Mr. Welch unlike Konosuke was not a founder. The age difference of the two is roughly 40 years, (Matsushita being the elder) this fact cannot be unrelated. In America, the waves of England's industrial revolution were making its impact. Of course, I have absolutely no intention of narrating the history, and current status of Panasonic and GE. However, there is an interesting aspect to the next generation of these two gentlemen, although there was Jeff Immelt, and Masaharu Matsushita, the two 'Gods' were not satisfied. This is an interesting common factor. Konosuke was notorious in his approaches toward reform, in 1977

イメルト氏(Jeff Immelt)、松下正治氏という方々が居たが、二人の神様は満足していなかった。面白い共通点ではある。松下翁には変革を導く非情があり、1977年には旧制工業学校卒の山下俊彦を25人抜きで3代目社長に任命している——有名な山下跳びである。

2017年、米国にトランプ大統領が誕生し、米朝関係に電撃的な変革を実現しようとしている。GEとパナソニックにも、経営の舵取りを新感覚で行うという強者が、期せずして現れた。GEにジョン・フラナリー氏(John Flannery)とパナソニックの津賀一宏氏である。両者には共通点がある。肯定的な共通点と否定的な共通点である。

先ず肯定的な共通点は、共に動かない物(製品・資産)から動く物(製品・資産)へと変える。GEの場合、約10のビジネス・ユニットのうち7ユニットが成果あり、3ユニットがロス・メーキング(Loss making)である。この10ユニットを縦割り(サイロ)ではなく横の関連性を持たせるように変える。エンジン(航空)、医療機器、電力に絞って技術の共通性を生かす。一方、パナソニックの津賀氏は白物(家電製品——動かない製品の典型である)から動く製品にシフトする。すなわち自転車や自動車である。自転車は解るが、自動車で何をするのか解らなかった。よく見ると強力で長持ちする電池の開発のようである。世界で最も多い海水を思うと水の分解で水素を創る方向に行くような感じがする。水素電池が良さそうである。燃焼すれば水になるだけである。役員の数を減らすのも、よい共通点である。今流行の働き方改革も両社共にきめ細かくコストカットを行っている。

さて、否定的な共通点。これが結構ある。先ず経理処理の問題を両社共に抱えている。筆者はこの専門性はないので、コメントは控えたい。また売上げ・利益も共に落ちている。

今後の課題として気がかりなことを申し上げたい。それは各事業部門に自立性(Autonomy)を、どのような形で——独立採算？　どのように実行して行くのか——ロス・メーキングなら首？　など少し長い目で眺めてみたい。両者とも成功を祈りたいからである。

he appointed Toshihiko Yamashita, a graduate of an old-system institute of technology, as the third president, frog-leaping 25 other potential candidates, this unorthodox appointment became famous as Yamashita's leap.

In America, President Trump was elected, and we can see that the realization of the United States and Korea relationship is taking on a drastic transformation. Within both GE and Panasonic, taking the helm of running the business with new and innovative sense two strong individuals appeared. The individuals are; in GE, John Flannery, and in Panasonic, Kazuhiro Tsuga. These two share common factors, both positive common factors and negative common factors.

Let us first look at the positive common factor, their change of stationary items (products/assets) to mobile items (products/assets). In the case of GE, 7 out of 10 business units were showing results, the remaining 3 units were loss making. Instead of viewing the 10 units as silo, or vertical structures, a change was made to establish a relationship between the units in a horizontal fashion. Narrowing down business areas to; engines (aircraft), medical devices, electricity, while utilizing the similarity of technology to each sector. In the case of Panasonic, Mr. Tsuga shifted from home electric appliances to mobile products. Resulting in a move toward bicycles and automobiles. Bicycles were understandable, but it was a puzzle as to what the intentions were in automobiles. An observation made it clear that it was the development of a strong and durable battery. Globally, looking at the most abundant water source which is sea water, through a decomposition process of this water, there is a potential to produce hydrogen. A hydrogen battery looks promising. When combusted the by-product is just water. Decreasing the number of executives is also a common factor among the two. In terms of negative common factors of the two, both individuals are extremely focused on cutting costs, as well as attentive toward policies on the current trend of the way their employees work, which is appropriate. Both corporations are faced with issues surrounding accounting. In view that I am not a specialist in this area, I will avoid commenting further on this. In addition, both sales and profit are decreasing.

I would like to mention issues that are foreseen in the future. What will the structure look like to assure the autonomy of each individual business division to ensure that they will be independently profitable? How will the process take place, getting fired if you are in a loss-making unit? I would like to take a long-term view on their progress, for I pray for both firm's success.

# 第９話

初出：2018年8月27日

# 望月

© EEN CORPORATION/amanaimages

正確には陰暦15日の満月のことであるが、藤原道長（966年～1028年）52歳の秋（旧暦10月16日、1018年）、「この世をば　わが世とぞ思ふ　望月の　欠けたることも　なしと思へば」と詠んだ。当時、左大臣であった道長は、今なら内閣総理大臣にして首相というところか。3人の天皇の外祖父となった有頂天の道長が、そこに居そうな感じがする。まあー、ここに藤原官僚政治が始まったのである。ちょうど聖徳太子の懐刀であった藤原不比等から16代である。その藤原官僚政治は、近くは明治維新（1868年）まで続いたのである。朝廷、官僚そして幕府（将軍）、その役割分担は…？　後で触れることにして、先を急ごう。藤原五摂家の筆頭である近衛文麿は太平洋戦争の責任を取り、自決をした（1945年）。それでも、太平洋戦争前の近衛氏は、東の鎌倉と言われた白樺派の我孫子市に別荘を持ち、庭先にはゴルフ場を持ち（現在の我孫子ゴルフ倶楽部）、かの市丸姐さんとの蜜月を楽しんだと言われている。

さて月というと、いろいろな顔を見せてくれる。筆者と家内の生涯で最も悲しい日であった5月19日（1990年）の月は、涙を流しているような半欠けの上弦の月であった。この月は、生涯脳裏から消えることは無い。忘れられない満月も何度か経験した。箱根の山の上ホテルの部屋から、家内と見た月は忘れられない。黄金に輝く満月であった。そして南

## Narrative 9

# Mochizuki (the meaning of the Full Moon)

© coward_lion - stock.adobe.com

Accurately, within the lunar calendar (a calendar based upon the monthly cycles of the Moon's phases) although the 15th represents a full moon, Fujiwara no Michinaga (966～1028) in the autumn when he was of 52 years old(Japan's old lunisolar calendar October, 16th, 1018) composed the poem, or 'waka',[Kono Yo Ba Waga Yo ToZo Omou Mochizuki No Keketaru Koto Mo Nashi To Omoe Ba]in which Michinaga compares the perfection of the full moon to his own accomplishments. At the time, Michinaga was what in current terms, was in the political position of prime minister. Becoming the maternal grandfather of three emperors, it is as though the ecstatic Michinaga is right before us. Well, this is the beginning of Fujiwara's bureaucratic politics. He is just at the 16th generation from Fujiwara no Fuhito, who is known as the right-hand advisor to Shotoku Taishi. Fujiwara's bureaucratic politics continued until as recently to the Meiji Restoration (1868). What were the roles allotted to; the Imperial Court, bureaucracy, and shogunate government (shogun)? This will be touched upon later, let us proceed. A primacy of the five families of the Fujiwara clan is Fumimaro Konoe, who taking responsibility for the Pacific War, committed suicide (1945). Prior to the Pacific War, Mr. Konoe, possessed a vacation home in an area what known as the eastern Kamakura and home to the Shirakabaha (literary circle), Abiko City, with a golf course in the front lawn (the present Abiko Golf Club), where it is said that the renown performer Ichimarune enjoyed a close relationship.

Speaking of the moon, it shows us a variety of faces. On what was the saddest day for my wife and myself, May 19th (1990) the half missing waning moon in its first quarter looked as though it was shedding tears. This moon will remain forever in my mind as long as I live. I have

半球オーストラリアの満月、トルコのアナトリアの高原をドライブ中に見え隠れする満月は見事であった。どこまで付いて来るの？　いや自分が追っかけているくせに！

ところで、黄金色や緑黄金色の発色に成功し、その月を仕上げたチタン芸術品を生み出している芸術作家が居るのを御存じだろうか。藤川哲也氏である。藤川氏は東京都出身で家業の金属加工業・藤川製作所を承継し、1988年にチタンの研究を開始した。チタンアーティストとして「煌彩色（こうさいしょく）」と呼ばれるを色合いを生み出した。煌彩色とは、自然色（七色）を光・場・時間軸をもとに変化（へんげ）させたような色合いである。筆者も、月をモチーフとしての黄金色の月、緑黄金色の月やダビデの星などの製作をお願いし、そのチタンアート作品の何とも言えぬ煌彩色を楽しんでいる。藤川氏は「ロイヤルパークホテルズ ザ 羽田アート公募展」に入選および入賞を果たしている。現在、神奈川県小田原市国府津にチタンアート「アノニム工房」を開設している。

さて、朝廷、官僚と幕府という三極の役割分担はどうだったのだろうか考えてみたい。朝廷は雲上人として昼夜逆の風流な生活を楽しんでいたのだろうが、結局は藤原五摂家の官僚が支えていたのだろう。外祖父として見返りが大きいし、一方、朝廷は万世一系を明治維新まで維持できたのである。それでは、官僚を支えてきたのは誰かというと幕府である。官僚は形の上では朝廷と幕府に仕えていたが、幕府の中に取り込まれていたのである。もちろん朝廷の中にもしたたかな公家もおり、幕府の強者：勝・西郷と共に公武合体などという「離れ業」をやれる者もいたのも、皆様ご存じの通りである。

それもつかの間、明治維新により天皇親政となって藤原家官僚はお役御免となり、明治天皇により新官僚が任命された。目指したのは、当時の先進国欧米に学び、追いつき、追い越せであった。現在の霞が関官僚の実力は仏国・英国官僚と並んで、世界有数のシンクタンク（Think Tank）となっている。

also experienced numerous unforgettable full moons. I will not forget the full moon that my wife and I saw from our room at the Yama No Ue Hotel of Hakone. It was a gleaming gold full moon. Then there is the southern hemisphere Australia's full moon, and the spectacular full moon I saw during the drive through Turkey's Anatolia highlands. To what extent is it going to follow me? When in fact it is I who is pursuing it.

Are you aware that there is an artist who has succeeded in capturing the golden or greenish golden color of the moon through his titanium objects of art? It is Tetsuya Fujikawa. Mr. Fujikawa, a native of Tokyo who succeeded the family's metal processing business; the Fujikawa Factory, and in 1988 started research into titanium. As a titanium artist he developed a glistening textured pigment. This glistening, metallic textured pigment taken from the natural colors (seven colors), provides an alteration of light, place and time. I, myself have placed orders for several pieces; one with a motif of a golden colored moon, a greenish golden moon, and one with the star of David, I thoroughly enjoy the sheen of the glistening metallic texture of these titanium art objects. Mr. Fujikawa has succeeded in being selected and awarded in the Royal Park Hotel's the Haneda Art exhibition. Currently, on show at the titanium art [Anonium Workshop] located in Kozu, Odawara City, Kanagawa Prefecture.

Now, let us think of the roles allotted Imperial Court, bureaucracy and shogunate government. The Imperial Court is perceived as an environ where the privileged; those who presided on clouds, enjoyed a lifestyle that day was night, and night was day, ultimately were most likely being supported by bureaucrats such as the five families of the Fujiwara clan. As the rewards of being the maternal grandfather must have indeed been significant, and to add to this, the Imperial Court is an unbroken line of reign which continued until the Meiji Restoration. So, who was it that supported the bureaucracy, it was the shogunate government. Although in its structural formation, the bureaucracy was to serve both the Imperial Court and the shogunate government, however, it was absorbed, or taken in by the shogunate government. Of course, there were scrupulous and formidable nobility within the Imperial Court, with shogunate men of influence such as; Katsu and Saigo, pulled off in establishing a union between the Imperial Court and the shogunate government, as many of you are aware.

This maneuver was short lived, for with the Meiji Restoration, a new government directly under the Emperor was established in which the Emperor Meiji newly appointed bureaucrats, bringing the Fujiwara clan bureaucracy to an end. The goal was to, learn from, catch up to and overtake, the developed western nations of the time. The capability of current bureaucrats in Kasumigaseki equal that of their French and English counterparts, proving to be one of the world's most effective Think Tanks.

## 第10話　　初出：2018年9月10日

# 壁を壊した二人

© Abaca/amanaimages

*Mikhail Sergeevich Gorbachev*
ミハイル・セルゲーエヴィチ・ゴルバチョフ

壁を壊したと言えば、ゴルバチョフ氏とトランプ氏である。ミハイル・ゴルバチョフ（1931年〜）氏は、ベルリンの壁を壊す切っ掛けを、当時西ドイツの首相であったコール氏（ヘルムート・コール、1930年〜2017年）と共につくった（1989年）。ドナルド・トランプ氏（1946年〜）は、韓国と北朝鮮の見えない壁を壊す切っ掛けを、韓国の文在寅大統領（1953年〜）と共につくった（2018年）。共に世界を変える成果である。

ゴルバチョフ氏がグラスノスチ（情報公開）、ペレストロイカ（改革）そしてベルリンの壁の崩壊と進めた裏には、厳しい祖父の体験が影響している気がする。スターリン時代の高級官僚であった祖父がスターリンの逆鱗に触れ、粛清にあい投獄。以来一家はコルホーズの農民となり、ゴルバチョフ氏も農民の子として育った。氏の茶目っ気な性格からして、クラスでは人気者であり、先生のお気に入りだったに違いない。後にモスクワ大学の法学部に入学（19歳、1950年）。そこで知り合ったライーサと結婚（1953年）した。

1985年、共産党書記長に就任するとグラスノスチを実行して、1988年には幹部会議長に就任。ソ連邦における権力の確立である。

## Narrative 10

# The Two Who Brought Down the Wall

© Polaris/amanaimages

*George Herbert Walker Bush*
ジョージ・H・W・ブッシュ
第41代アメリカ合衆国大統領

When I think of bringing down a wall, Mr. Gorbachev and Mr. Trump comes to mind. Mikhail Gorbachev(1931～) in 1990, he initiated events that would lead to the fall of the Berlin Wall with the then Chancellor of Germany, Helmut Kohl (1930～2017). Donald Trump(1946～)in 2018, broke through the invisible wall between Korea and North Korea, together with Korea's President Moon Jaen-in(1953～), changing the world.

Mr. Gorbachev, I believe that there may be a hidden aspect behind his policy of Glasnost (openness and transparency), Perestroika (restructuring), and ultimately the fall of the Berlin Wall, which could have been influenced by what his strict grandfather had experienced. During the rule of Stalin, his grandfather was a high-ranking government official who had angered Stalin, which resulted in his expulsion and imprisonment. From this event, the family became collective farmers, Gorbachev was raised as a farmer's child. Possessing a playful and mischievous spirit, he was popular in his class, most likely the teacher's favorite. In 1950, at the age of 19, he went on to study at Moscow University's Law Department, where he met Raisa. The two were married in 1953. Gorbachev initiated Glasnost, and in 1988 was appointed as Chairman of the Presidium of the Supreme Soviet, securing his authority within the Soviet Union.

When I think of the fall of the Berlin Wall, I recall the 1963 speech by U.S. President Kennedy in front of the Berlin Wall directed at East Germany, German people breaking the wall (1989), and the televised broadcast image of a shot through the broken wall showing East Germany's Triumphal Arch.

ベルリンの壁崩壊で思い出すのは、米国ケネディー大統領が壁の前で東ドイツに向けて行った演説（1963年）、壁を打ち砕くドイツの人々の姿（1989年）、そしてTVの生放送で見た壊された壁を通して見た東ドイツ側の凱旋門である。

筆者は、壁崩壊前の西ベルリンを3度程学会出席のため訪問している。実に安全で素晴らしい街であった。ブラント市長（在任期間1957年〜1966年、後に西ドイツ大統領）の時代である。

ゴルバチョフ氏に話を戻そう。氏は、1985年に新しくペレストロイカという改革路線を打ち出した。氏はゴルビーと愛称され、かの英国首相サッチャー女史をして「この男となら話せる」と言わしめたのは有名な話である。

そして1989年12月には、米国大統領ブッシュ（父）とマルタ会談で「冷戦の終結」を宣言している。まさに、時が追いつかないようなスピードである。

一方、国内では、経済は必ずしも上手く行っておらず、共産党支配を改めて大統領制を決め、自ら初代大統領となった（1990年）。共産党の保守派がクーデターを起こし、ゴルバチョフ氏は一時監禁されたが、クーデターは失敗した。

ご存じのようにゴルビーは、いまだ世界を飛び回り、大の親日家でもある。

さてもう一人見えぬ壁を崩壊させたのは、米国大統領トランプ氏である。2018年6月11日、シンガポールで北朝鮮の最高指導者である金正恩氏と面会し、氏を世界に紹介したのは記憶に新しい。詳細に触れるつもりはないが、国務長官ポンペオ氏に期待をして止まない。

トランプ大統領が若くして成績優秀／神童であったのはよく知られている。大人になっては、名門・ペンシルバニア大学ウォートン校（Wharton）を卒業している。同校は世界トップレベルのビジネススクールである。彼の息子たち、そして娘のイヴァンカ（Ivanka）とその夫であるクッシュナー（Kushner）の優秀さは、その容姿を含め、言を俟たない。

Prior to the fall of the Berlin Wall, I visited West Berlin 3 times to attend conferences. I found the city to be safe and absolutely wonderful. My visits coincided with the period that Willy Brandt was the Governing Mayor of Berlin (1957-1966) who later became the Chancellor of Germany.

Returning to Mr. Gorbachev, in 1985 he introduced a new Perestroika reform policy.

Widely known as 'Gorby', there is a famous episode in which the renown former Prime Minister of England, Margaret Thatcher was said to have stated "I can talk with this man."

Then in December of 1989, he jointly declared the end of the Cold War with U.S. President George H.W. Bush at the Malta Summit. Undoubtedly at a speed that time could not keep up with.

On the other hand domestically, the economy was not performing as expected, he presented the idea to repealing the Communist Party as the 'ruling party', as well as introducing the role of head of government to a presidency, which he became the first elected president in 1990. Senior members of the Communist Party launched a coup d'état, leading to Gorbachev being placed under house arrest, however the coup was failed.

As many are aware, Gorby continues to travel around the world, and is a great Japanophile.

Another individual who initiated the destruction of an invisible wall is U.S. President Trump. Fresh on everyone's memory is the meeting of June 11th of this year (2019) in Singapore, where he met with North Korea's Supreme Leader, Kim Jong-un in Singapore, introducing the reclusive leader to the world. Although I will avoid going into the finer details, I hold great expectations toward U.S. Secretary of State, Mr. Pompeo.

It is widely known that President Trump excelled academically; a child prodigy. He went on to graduate from the Wharton School at the University of Pennsylvania, which is highly regarded as one of the best business academic institutions. The superb intellect and handsome appearance of his sons, daughter, Ivanka and her husband, Mr. Kushner is undoubtable.

第11話　初出：2018年12月10日

# 両断 ――分断

*Ryunosuke Akutagawa*
芥川龍之介
(1892～1927)

© 文藝春秋/アマナイメージズ

両断といえば、一刀両断とくる。武士の言葉であると思っていたが、どうも人を切る話でもなさそうである。むしろ、芥川龍之介や太宰治が使ったように早く決断するという意味が多いような気がする。もちろん、二つに分けるという言葉でもある。分断である。

剣術の流れでは、一刀流、二刀流がある。人の腕は2本だから、さすが三刀流はない。二刀流では宮本武蔵が有名で、一刀流の吉岡道場そして佐々木小次郎との対決は有名だ。

野球にも二刀流がある。ベーブ・ルース（米国大リーグ、George Herman "Babe" Ruth Jr. 、1895年2月6日～1948年8月16日）や日本プロ野球から米国大リーグに移った我らが大谷翔平君である。人柄と実力からか、米国でも大変な人気である。

さて、筆者は米国2018年11月6日（火曜日）の中間選挙（Midterm Election）前の11月2日午後7時に「米国中間選挙で、共和党は負けないことに賭けたい」と本誌編集当局に伝えておいた。確かに共和党は負け

## Narrative 11

# Bisection - Fragmentation

*Osamu Dazai*
太宰 治
(1909 ~ 1948)



When Japanese hear the term 'ryodan', meaning to bisect, the phrase 'Itto ryodan' comes to mind. The Japanese characters used to reflect this phrase is 'one sword bisection'. Although I believe this phrase is a samurai term, it does not necessarily reflect the gruesome act of cutting an opponent in half. On the contrary, as utilized by renown authors such as; Ryunosuke Akutagawa and Osamu Dazai, I feel that the meaning of this phrase is to express a speedy decision. Of course, the phrase also has the meaning of making two parts of a whole. Thus, fragmentation.

In the realm of sword fencing, there is the one-sword discipline and two-sword discipline. We humans only have two arms, naturally, there a three-sword discipline does not exist. In the two-sword discipline, Musashi Miyamoto is well known, as in the famous confrontation Kojiro Sasaki who represented the one-sword Yoshioka School.

Baseball also possesses the two-sword discipline. U.S. Major Leaguer, George Herman 'Babe' Ruth Jr. (February 6, 1895 – August 16, 1948) as well as Shohei Otani, who after playing in the Japanese professional baseball league, became a player of the U.S. Major League. His personality and capability has earned him great popularity in the United States.

Prior to the November 6th U.S. Mid-term Elections, I had notified the publishers of this book, that I had made a bet on November 2nd at 7 P.M., that the Republicans will not lose. I

なかった。しかし、何とトランプ氏は翌日11月8日「大成功／Tremendous success」と宣った。もっとも、上院は一人増やしているし、恐れ入りました。しかし、氏の「アメリカ第一／America First」政策の結果、図らずも分断が起きているのは困ったものである。たぶんトランプ氏はこれから二期目を目指して頑張りを見せるので、トランプ後の新大統領が2020年か2024年か、共和党か民主党かの興味も含めて、選ばれた新大統領の力量が将来の米国を決定づけることになるであろう。民主党も厳しい分断が続いている。左派サンダース氏(Sanders)はまだ人気があり、2020年の大統領選にも間違いなく立候補する。保守派のブルームバーグ氏(Bloomberg)も立候補宣言し、ヒラリー女史も再考中とか。分裂民主に勝ち目があるのか、はなはだ疑問である。

中国の国家主席習近平氏(Chinese President Xi Jinping)もトランプ氏(President Trump)の米国とアジア諸国との関係分断に躍起になって動いている。一帯一路(One Belt and One Road)はまさにその手段である。一党(共産党)支配と監視社会を統治モデルとして強要されるので、アセアン諸国などは敬遠しがちになり、必ずしも一帯一路は順調でなく、分断はそれほど成功していない。一方で習氏はアフリカにも目を付け巨額援助をすることで、従来の英国やEU関係国とアフリカ諸国との分断に成功している。

最近の韓国文大統領の日本に対する発言は、明らかに日米連携の分断を狙ったもので、だれが後ろにいるかは自明である。朝鮮半島の問題が解決となると、その地域を支配するのは日米である。韓国文大統領が頼り、日米に楔を打ちたい中国国家主席習氏が入り込んでくる。文大統領は覚悟を決めて関わらないと、日米分断の心算が自滅の運命をたどることになるだろう。韓国知識人や民衆がそれに気付き始めている。

一方で、習氏による国内開発のスピードは素晴らしく、従来の発想を超えた都市構造モデルが進んでいる。広い道路と駐車スペースなど。彼の夢は、7〜8世紀の長安(世界一の国際都市)の再来である。その手段は一帯一路である。一方で国内は分断解消とはいかに。

won my bet, for indeed, the Republicans did not lose. On the following day, November 8th, Mr. Trump declared [A tremendous success]. Of course, the Republicans succeeded in adding another member to the Senate, impressive. However, Mr. Trump's administrative "America First" strategy, has unfortunately resulted in fragmentation. It is very likely that President Trump is directing his energy toward being re-elected for a second-term, the new president after Trump, whether it will be 2020 or 2024, including the interest toward whether it is the Democratic Party, or Republican Party, the ability of the elected new president will determine the future of the United States. The Democratic Party's difficult fragmentation continues. Left-wing Sanders is still popular, and there is no doubt that he will become a candidate in the 2020 presidential elections. The conservative Bloomberg has announced his candidacy, and it is said that Hilary is in a state of reconsideration. As to whether the fragmentated Democratic Party can win, is extremely doubtful.

Chinese President Xi Jinping is feverishly motivated to see that President Trump American and Asian nations relationship becomes fragmented. The One Belt One Road Initiative is precisely one of his methods. There is an overall elusion within Asian nations toward the very possible enforcement of China's governing model of one ruling party (Communist Party) and a highly monitored society, thus hindering the progress of the One Belt One Road Initiative, reflecting that fragmentation is not necessarily succeeding. President Xi has set his eyes on Africa, and through the provision of enormous sums of aid, is succeeding in fragmenting relationships that were previously established between the U.K. and EU countries and African nations.

Recent statements toward Japan, by South Korea President Moon are clearly aimed at fragmenting the U.S.-Japan relationship, who exactly is behind this is very clear. If the Korean Peninsula issue is resolved, the area will be controlled by Japan and the U.S. It all depends on South Korea President Moon, in the event a wedge is driven between U.S.-Japan, as Chinese President Xi hopes, he will not hesitate in entering the region. If President Moon does not get involved with determination, the intended outcome of the fragmentation of U.S.-Japan relations will lead to a fate of self-destruction. South Korean intellectuals and the public are starting to realize this.

On the other hand, the speed of President Xi's domestic development is amazing, metropolitan mechanism model exceeds prior ideas. Such as, wide streets and parking space. His dream is to resurrect the 7th ~ 8th century ancient capital of Cháng'ān (the world's largest international city). The method to do so is the One Belt One Road Initiative. Domestically, resolving fragmentation is unsuccessful.

# 第12話

初出：2018年12月24日

# カルロス ゴーン(Carlos Ghosn)氏は何をしたのか

© Sipa USA/amanaimages

*Carlos Ghosn*
ゴーン、おまえもか！

2018年11月20日(火曜日)午前11時である。ゴーン氏は11月19日未明に羽田空港で東京地検特捜部に逮捕された。司法取引があったという。氏にとって寝耳に水だったようである。同日、日仏文化交流会が開かれており、ゴーン氏はそのキー・ノート・スピーカーとして来日したと言われている。青天の霹靂とはこのことか。

筆者がゴーン氏に最初に触れたのは、2009年ゴーン氏が鉄鋼業界の再編につながる切っ掛けを作った時である。従来鉄鋼業界と自動車メーカーの間には、ある鉄鋼会社とある自動車メーカーが自動車用鋼板の購入を行う風習があった。ゴーン氏は、日産の自動車用鋼板の取引先を絞り、必要量かつ的確な品質の鋼板の購入を始めたのだ。仕来りと価格の破壊である。氏の英断に賛同した記事を書いた覚えがある。ゴーン氏のおかげで日本の鉄鋼業界の構造改革が進み、日本の鉄鋼会社のＭ＆Ａを狙っていたインドのタタ製鉄との競争にも耐えられるようになったのである。日本の鉄鋼業界関係の人なら覚えているはずである。

ゴーン氏はルノー(Renault)・日産・三菱自動車の会長として辣腕を振るい、3社連合の世界売上げ台数は世界第2位を達成した(2017年)。このような環境の中で個人の蓄財を重ねているうちに、雇われ社長で

Narrative 12

# What did Carlos Ghosn do?

It is now Tuesday, November 20th, 11A.M. Carlos Ghosn was arrested at Haneda Airport in the early morning hours of November 19th, 2018 by the Tokyo District Prosecutions Special Search Department. It is said that a judicial transaction had taken place. This had come as a complete surprise to Mr. Ghosn. On this very same day of his arrest, Mr. Ghosn was to attend a Japan-France cultural exchange event, where he was to be the key note speaker, which was the reason for his visit to Japan. The turn of events must have come as a bolt out of the blue.

The first time I touched upon the subject of Mr. Ghosn was in 2009 when he presented an opportunity for the steel industry to restructure. Conventionally, it was customary for a specific car maker to purchase steel sheets for automobile manufacturing, from a specific steel company. Mr. Ghosn narrowed down the steel firms from which steel plates would be purchased for Nissan automobiles, he started to purchase the necessary quantity with a precision toward quality. This was a destruction of tradition and price. I recall writing about how I approved of his decisive judgement. It was through Mr. Ghosn that the structural reform of Japan's steel industry progressed, allowing the industry to endure the competition of India's Tata Steel, which had the M&A of Japanese steel firms in its sights. This is most likely well remembered by those who are involved with the Japanese steel industry.

Mr. Ghosn reflected his shrewd capability as the chairman for Renault, Nissan and Mitsubishi Motors, accomplishing, in 2017, the three-company alliance, second place in the number of global car sales. It was within this environment, repeatedly accumulating his personal wealth, forgetting that he was hired president, had envisioned himself as the owner of the firm (s). This is the mistake.

It also appears that he was good with women. Last year he held his third marriage ceremony at the Palace of Versailles, which is said to have been rented out at the company's expense. If this is true, this is also a mistake.

The reaction from France. Renault, did not dismiss Mr. Ghosn as CEO and Chairman. In addition, the President of France, Emmanuel Macron immediately dispatched the French

あったことを忘れ、オーナー気分になってしまったのだ。これは間違いである。

氏は女性にも腕がよかったようで…。2016年の3度目の結婚式は、なんとヴェルサイユ宮殿の会社持ち貸し切りと言われている。事実とすれば、これも間違いである。

さて、フランスの対応である。ルノーは、氏をCEO／会長から解任しなかった。さらにマクロン首相は駐日本大使ローラン・ピック（Laurent Pic）を直ちにゴーン氏の弁護士と会わせている。もちろん何を語ったかは誰も知る由もない。弁護士を通して、ゴーン氏が法的に戦う意思表示をしたというので、氏の日本における功罪をどのように評価するのか、興味深い。筆者は氏の功の部分を今でも高く評価したい。勾留も長引きそうだし、裁判は長期戦間違いなしである。最終不起訴（無罪）を勝ち取るまでやるであろう。一般的興味としては、保釈金と誰が身元引け請け人であるか。おそらく、ゼロか数十億円、そして引受人はレバノン大使あたりかと思う。

最近、氏の生い立ちを読む機会があった。レバノン（Lebanon）移民の子としてブラジル（Brazil）で生まれている。国籍はブラジル・フランス・レバノンである。出身校は、フランスの著名な官僚育成機関の一つであるパリ国立高等鉱業学校である。最古のフランスの高等教育機関の一つであり、ノーベル賞受賞者を２人（物理と経済）出している名門である。英国のオックスブリッジ（Oxbridge）や米国のIBリーグ（IB league）とは違った経歴であるが、パリやヨーロッパはまさに活躍の場である。それでも、氏には何か寂しげな影が付きまとう。何故だろうか、不思議である。

彼の合理主義／コストカッターは実にアメリカ的で、米国では氏の評判は悪くない。ニューヨークタイムズは11月19日、ゴーン氏が窮地に落ちたニッサンをいかに再生させたかをつづっている。なお、同日11月20日の西川社長の記者会見の様子は不可思議。氏も責任者ではなかったのか。

*Carlos Ghosn Portrait - Beirut*

Ambassador to Japan, Laurent Pic to meet with Mr. Ghosn's attorney. Of course, nobody is aware of what discussed at this meeting. Through his attorney, we learned that Mr. Ghosn was determined to fight in the court of law, it would be interesting to hear his evaluation of Japan's merits and demerits. I still would like to highly evaluate his merits. It looked as though his detention period would be extended, and there is no doubt that the trial will be a lengthy battle. He will probably fight until he finally wins a non-prosecution, (not guilty) verdict. The general interest is toward the bail amount and who will be his guarantor. The bail could possibly be zero or several billion yen, perhaps his guarantor could be the Lebanese Ambassador.

Recently, I had the opportunity to read about Mr. Ghosn's background. He was born in Brazil as a child to Lebanese immigrants. He sustains Brazilian, French and Lebanese nationalities. Academically he graduated from France's renown Ecole des Mines de Paris, which is regarded as a learning institution that prepares students for positions in government. One of the oldest and prestigious secondary academic institutions of France, that have within its alumni two Nobel Prize laureates (physics and economics). Although it may differ from England's Oxbridge and the Ivy League institutions of the United States, it is ideal for those who are active in Paris and Europe. Regardless of his amazing accomplishments, a veil of loneliness continuously surrounds him. What breeds this, is a mystery.

His rationalism and cost-cutting methods are truly American in nature, his reputation in the U.S. it not bad. The New York Times, in its November 19th article reports on how Mr. Ghosn revitalized Nissan when it was in trouble. In addition, on the same day, November 20th a press conference was held in which Nissan's president Nishikawa immitted a strange impression. Wasn't he also in a position of due diligence?

# 第13話

初出：2019年9月23日

# ミツコ――カレルギー伯爵夫人(チェコ)

© Mary Evans/amanaimages

*CASABLANCA*
「カサブランカ」

私のお気に入り俳優のハンフリー・ボガート(Humphrey Bogart)の映画カサブランカを思い出す。オールドファンには、ちょっと鼻にかかった声が懐かしい。相手役イングリッド・バーグマン(Ingrid Bergman)とのラブロマンスである。そして小柄なルノー署長役のクロード・レインズ(Claude Rains)の粋な計らい。飛行機はリスボンに向け離陸する。その時、若い東洋人が居たのをご記憶かと、彼こそミツコの次男リヒャルト(日本名・栄次郎、1894年～1972年)である。当時のドイツを巡るヨーロッパ内の意見の相違を回避するのも、映画製作者の主旨の1つであった。そして現実にそのような動きをしていたのが、栄次郎であった。

何故、栄次郎はそういう行動をとることになったのか。興味深い。それは、ミツコ(1874年～1941年)と夫のカレルギー伯爵(Heinrich Coudenhove-Kalergi、1859年～1906年)の教育であろう。彼女は18歳の時、日本で結婚し7人の子宝にも恵まれた。彼女が近くのオーストリア・ハンガリー大使館に遊びに行くうちにカレルギー伯爵(大使)と出会い恋に落ち、国際結婚をする。伯爵は、天才肌の方で博愛にして語学の天才、

## Narrative 13

# Mitsuko Countess of Coudenhove-Kalergi (Czech)

© alamy/amanaimages

*A wedding photograph with her husband in 1892*

I am reminded of the film Casablanca, in which one of my favorite actors, Humphrey Bogart starred. Old fans will recall, with fond memory, the particular nasal quality of his voice. The film is a romantic drama with co-star Ingrid Bergman. Then there was the small in build, Claude Rains, in the part of police Captain Renault, who provides rather crafty arrangements. The aircraft takes off for Lisbon. At that time, some of you may recall the presence a young oriental man, he is in fact the younger son of Mitsuko, Richard (Japanese name; Eijiro, 1894~1972). This inclusion was made on the part of the film's producers, in avoiding the differences of opinions in Europe surrounding Germany at the time, was one of the points to be made in the film. In reality, this was something Eijiro was striving to do.

What was it that drove Eijiro to do so? This is quite interesting. It may stem from how Mitsuko (1874~1941) and her husband, Count Heinrich Coudenhove-Kalergi (1859~1906) had educated their children. When she was 18 years old, she was married in Japan and was

18カ国語を話したという。一方の彼女は骨董店のお嬢様であったが、せいぜい小学校程度の知識しかなかった。結婚をして伯爵が帰任したボヘミアとハンガリーにわたる広大な敷地に住み、改めて自分の無学を自覚し、家庭教師を仕事ごとに雇い勉学に励み、見事に伯爵夫人として自信と威厳を持って尊敬されるまでになったのである。二人並んだ写真を見ると、お見事伯爵夫人！と声をかけたくなる。

東京で生まれた長男・光太郎(ミヒャエル、1893年〜没年不詳)、次男・栄次郎も、母国に帰っても母ミツコの良妻賢母ぶりを見て育ったに違いない。そして日本に居た時、明治天皇の"四方の海　皆同胞と思う世に　など波風の　立ちさわぐらん"を聞かされていたに違いない。現実にその主旨を理解して後に動いたのが、前述の次男・栄次郎である。1923年には"汎ヨーロッパ"を著し、当時のドイツを巡る意見の相違の調停をしようとしていたのである。これが後のEEC(1958年発足)、EC(1967年発足)そしてEU(1993年発足)へと発展して行くのを見ると、栄次郎の活動はものすごいもので、伯爵夫人ミツコはもちろん、日本人としても大変な誇りである。伯爵夫人ミツコが、現在の世界の共生、グローバリゼーションの生みの親である。

一方、長男の光太郎は伯爵家の復興に専念していた。多分、父カレルギー伯爵の長男として家を守る責任・義務を見ていたのと、当時の日本の文化である家長主義がミツコの子供教育のなかにあったのかもしれない。現市長によると、残念なことに光太郎のお城は廃墟に近いという。

ドイツを巡る対立を解消しようとしていた次男・栄次郎も、第二次世界大戦(1939年〜1945年)が勃発、ヒトラーの登場ですべてがドイツ対ヨーロッパ連合軍となり、成す術(すべ)無し。これも天のミツコにとっても、残念であったろう。

ちなみに、日本でもよく知られた香水ミツコは、1919年にフランスのゲラン社(Guerlain)がパリで発売した。その名はカレルギー伯爵夫人ミツコから採ったという。今年は発売100周年になる。

blessed with 7 children. She had made visits to the Austro-Hungarian Embassy, located nearby, eventually meeting and falling in love with the Count (Ambassador), resulting in an international marriage. The Count, an extremely intelligent individual, said to be fluent in 16 languages, and a philanthropist. On the other hand, Mitsuko was the daughter of an antiques dealer, who at the times, would have had an elementary school level education at the best. Married to the Count and living within the vast estates of Bohemia Ronsperg, becoming aware of her limited education, she employed a number of tutors, studied hard, transforming into a magnificent countess embodying the dignity worthy of her rank, gaining the respect of those she encountered. Looking at the photograph of the couple, it encourages a salute of "Well done, Countess!"

The eldest son, Kohtaro (Johann 1983~1965) was born in Tokyo, the second son Eijiro, even with their return to their home country, was brought up through his mother Mitsuko's nature as a good wife and wise mother. When in Japan, must have had the opportunity to listen to Emperor Meiji's 'waka' (poem), "Yomo no Umi" (Surrounding Seas) in which he expresses; Thinking of the World, with Fellow countrymen, the Wind and Waves, are Rough, after understanding the meaning behind this poem, and taking action was the aforementioned, second son Eijiro. In 1923, he wrote his first book "Pan-Europa", striving to mediate the opinions that were surrounding Germany at the time. After which his movement for a united Europe developed into the; ECC (established 1958), EC (established 1967) and the EU (1993 established), the efforts of Eijiro was immense, Mitsuko, as well as the Japanese, we can be extremely proud. Countess Mitsuko was, in essence, the mother of the current world's unification, globalization.

On the other hand, the eldest son Kohtaro was dedicated in reviving the Count's estate. It is most likely, as the first-born son, he felt that it was responsibility and duty to defend his father, Count Kalergi legacy, this sense of duty; the head of household principle, was taken from Japan of the time, and perhaps taught to him as a child by Mitsuko. According to the current Mayor, unfortunately, Kohtaro's castle is close to ruin.

Eijiro, who was striving to disperse the conflicts involving Germany, with the start of the Second World War (1939~1945), and the arrival of Hitler bringing about the conflict of Germany against a European united force, was totally helpless. To Mitsuko, in heaven, this must have been a most unfortunate turn of events.

On a note, the perfume 'Mitsuko', well known in Japan, was manufactured and sold in Paris by France's Guerlain in 1919. Named after the Countess Mitsuko Kalergi, this year marks its 100th anniversary.

## 第14話

初出：2019年11月11日

# 平清盛——天をも畏れぬ男

© Mary Evans/amanaimages

大蘇芳年『新形三十六怪撰』の平清盛

最近久しぶりに、平将門塚（通称、将門の首塚）を大手町に訪ねた。私の隣村に将門の城跡があり、子供の頃よく訪ねた。将門（生年不詳～940年）は桓武天皇の5世子孫（桓武平氏）であり、次女春姫を通して大正天皇につながっているという。

さて平清盛（1118年～1181年）は、1137年に肥後守となり1138年に結婚し、重盛、基盛の2男に恵まれた。平治の乱（1159年）では、藤原官僚そして源氏の大将源義朝を破り、朝廷の衛兵を任され平家政治の隆盛の始まりを告げたのである。時に、牛若丸（義経の幼少名）と源義朝夫人だった常盤御前を匿ったのは有名な話である。また親友でもあった平時忠の姉・時子を継室として迎え（1147年）、宗盛が誕生した。また安芸守にも任ぜられた清盛は瀬戸内海の制海権を握り、父・忠盛とともに西に向けて櫓をこぐことになる。妻の時子が後白河上皇の第一子である二条天皇の乳母となったことから、清盛は二条天皇の後見役となった。そして検非違使別当、中納言となる。朝廷が分裂した保元の乱では、後白河上皇方に味方し勝利に貢献。自らの病魔からの回復、後白河上皇と複雑な関係の継続を経て、大納言となる。義弟の時忠が“平氏にあらずんば人

## Narrative 14

# Taira No Kiyomori, a Man Fearless of Imperial Rule

© The Bridgeman Art Library/amanaimages

織田信長（平氏）

Recently, I made a visit to the mound commemorating Taira no Masakado (popularly known as the burial mound of Makakado' s head) located in Ohtemachi. A neighboring village of mine, are the remains of Masakado's castle, and when I was a child, I would make frequent visits there. Masakado (year of birth unknown ~ 940) and he is a direct decedent of Emperor Kanmu by five generations (Kanmu Heishi), and through his second daughter he is connected to Emperor Taisho.

Proceeding to Taira no Kiyomori (1118~1181), in the year 1137 became the Higo no Kami, and was married in 1138, blessed with two sons; Shigemori and Motomori. In the Heiji Rebellion (1159), he defeats the Fujiwara bureaucracy and leader of the Minamoto clan, Minamoto no Yoshitomo, which led to his becoming responsible for the imperial guards, enabling him a step toward establishing the posterity of the Heike politics. It was time when, a famous story in which he shelters, Ushiwaka Maru (childhood name of Yoshitsune) and the wife of Minamoto no Yoshitomo, Tokiwa Gozen. He also marries (1147), as his second wife, Tokiko, an elder sister of his close friend, Taira no Tokitada, and from this union, Munemori is born. Kiyomori was appointed Aki No Kami a position that allowed him dominance of the sea in the Seto Naikai area, and with his father Tadamori, started rowing the oar aiming for the west. Kiyomori's wife, Tokiko becoming wet nurse to Emperor Nijo, the retired emperor Go-Shirakawa's first son, Kiyomori was appointed as guardian to the Emperor Nijo. his rise in ranks and position, becoming an overseer of the judiciary, then on to becoming a vice-minister. The Hogen Rebellion, in which there was a division within the imperial court, Kiyomori supported retired emperor Go-Shirakawa, and contributed to the victory. After recovering from an illness, he continues his complex relationship with retired emperor Go-Shirakawa, becoming chief councilor of state. His brother-in-law, Tokitada once said; "If you are not a Taira, you are not a person" praising the Taira clan's prosperity, reminiscent of Fujiwara Michinaga's poem, "Kono Yo Ba Waga Yo ToZo Omou Mochizuki No Keketaru Koto Mo Nashi To Omoe

にあらず”と平家一門の栄華をたたえたと言われるが、藤原道長の“わが世をば…”を思い出させる出来事である。

有名な鹿ケ谷の陰謀が起こる。これを知った清盛は後白河上皇以外の関係者を処罰。

さらに後白河上皇にチャレンジ、親後白河上皇派の官職をすべて非後白河上皇派に編成替え。このようなご都合主義を安易にすると必ずつまずくのが世の常なるを気が付かなかった清盛は迂闊だったと言わざるを得ない。さらに後白河上皇を幽閉。1180年、娘の徳子との間にできた幼少の安徳天皇を即位させ、自らは外祖父となり、太政大臣(現在の総理大臣・首相)にまで上り詰めた。

とにかく若い頃の清盛はかなりの暴れん坊で比叡山に弓を弾き、長じても朝廷を畏れず福原に皇居(幼少の安徳天皇)を遷した。厳島には厳島神社を建立、有名な平家納経を献じている。このように見ると、よく筆者が口にする平家だからこそ出来る変革である。戦国時代の信長も平家であり、朝廷をなんとも思わぬ武家でもあった。しかし、興味があるのは清盛も信長も最後の成就を果たす前に無念の死を迎える運命だったことである。最近旅したマケドニアのアレキサンダー大王の死にも似た印象を受ける。時代が早すぎたのであろうか。

そして源平合戦である。これは、清盛の継室であった時子の情けが平家一門にとっては仇となったと筆者は見ている。あの時、頼朝、今若(出家)そして義経を生かしておかなかったら、この戦いはなかったであろう。清盛の死とともに、平家の滅亡はつるべ落としであった。そして壇ノ浦の戦いで平家は滅亡する。この時の時子の情けを逆参考にする事例は数知れない。徳川家康の淀君切り、徳川家光の秀頼切り……などなど。しかし、時子の情けは大いに称賛されるべきである。

また清盛で特筆すべきは、日宋貿易である。これも新しいことをする平家なるが故にできたことである。こうして得た輸入品、輸出品は双方に恩恵をもたらし鎌倉時代まで続いた。仏教経典も輸入され鎌倉仏教に影響を与えたという。

Bain which Michinaga compares the perfection of the full moon to his own accomplishments.

Then the famous Shishigatani conspiracy occurs. Learning of this, Kiyomori punishes those involved, except for the retired emperor Go-Shirakawa.

He further challenges the retired emperor Go-Shirakawa by replacing pro-Go-Shirakawa bureaucrats and appointing anti-Go-Shirakawa individuals to these posts, totally changing the composition. One must point out that Kiyomori not realizing that imposing these self-interest approaches easily, as a rule, inevitably has its consequences. In addition, he imprisoned the retired emperor Go-Shirakawa. In 1180, his daughter, Tokuko's infant son, (by marriage with Emperor Takakura), was installed as Emperor Antoku, ultimately making himself the grandfather to the Emperor, and ultimately securing the position of chief minister of the government, de factor administrator of the imperial government.

Kiyomori in his youth was in any case, a rowdy and challenging Hieizan, although advancing in age, he was fearless of the imperial court, moving the imperial palace (residence of the young Emperor Antoku) to Fukuhara. Erecting the Ikutsushima Shrine on Ikutsushima, where he dedicated the famous Heike clan copied sutras. Looking at these events, as I often say, it was only the Heike clan that could achieve such changes. Nobunaga of the Warring States Period, was of the Heike clan, a samurai who is also known for his disregard toward the imperial court. However, what is interesting is that both, Kiyomori and Nobunaga, die with regret prior to achieving their respective ambitions. This similarity of destiny was further impressed upon me with Alexander the Great's untimely death, that I pondered upon during my most recent travels to Macedonia. Perhaps they were all too early for their time.

Now the Genpei War. Personally, I believe that it was the sympathy shown by Kiyomori's second wife, Tokiko became an Achilles's heel for the Heike clan. At that crucial time, if Yoritomo (childhood name, Imawaka), and Yoshitune were not allowed to live, this battle would not have occurred. With the death of Kiyomori, the Heike clan's decline was rapid. The Battle of Dan No Ura, brought about the extinction of the Heike clan. In hindsight, there are countless examples of reverse reference toward Tokiko's sympathy. Tokugawa Ieyasu slaying Yodo Gimi, Tokugawa Iemitsu slaying Hideyori, etc. However, Tokiko's sympathy should be applauded.

What should be especially noted in regards to Kiyomori is the Japan-Song Dynasty trade. This endeavor, I believe could only be accomplished by the Heike, who enjoyed conducting new things. The goods that were imported, and exported were mutually beneficial, continuing into the Kamakura period. Buddhist sutras, literature was also imported, influencing Kamakura Buddhism.

第15話　　初出：2019年11月25日

# ジンギス汗——中原攻めから
# オスマントルコ帝国まで

© chiakto - stock.adobe.com

*genghis khan*
ジンギス汗

2006年9月にイスタンブールのインターコンチネンタルホテルで、フロントのスタッフの名札がフビライとある。Welcome Sirと挨拶され、答えて曰く、I am Genghis。Oh、my father！と来た。

しかし、調べてみると、2人ともいい加減だった。確かにモンゴル帝国を拡大したのは、ジンギス汗（Genghis Khan、1155年～1227年）であるが、最初の大汗はフビライ大汗（1215～1294年）である。ジンギス汗が有名なのは、彼が中国大陸を併合してモンゴル大帝国を完成させたことである。ジンギス汗の甥であるフビライ汗が首都をカラコルムから北に移し、北の京すなわち北京（ペキン）とした。

ジンギス汗は1162年にモンゴルの北部で父イェスゲイ（Yesugei）の本妻の長男として誕生。幼名をテムジン（Temujin）と称した。テムジンが9歳の時、父親は彼を新しい妻の家に移動。ところが、父親はライバルの他族の祭りに招かれた折毒殺された。早速、家に帰ったテムジンは、一門の長を名乗ろうとしたが、一門がこの若造を認めず。逆に一門から追放の浮き目に遭う。折りしも、狩りの分け前で口論となり、怒ったテムジンは異母弟を殺害。5年の幽閉の身になった。

## Narrative 15

# Genghis Khan

## ——Ruling from Zhong-yuan to the Ottoman Empire

© Peter Hermes Furian - stock.adobe.com

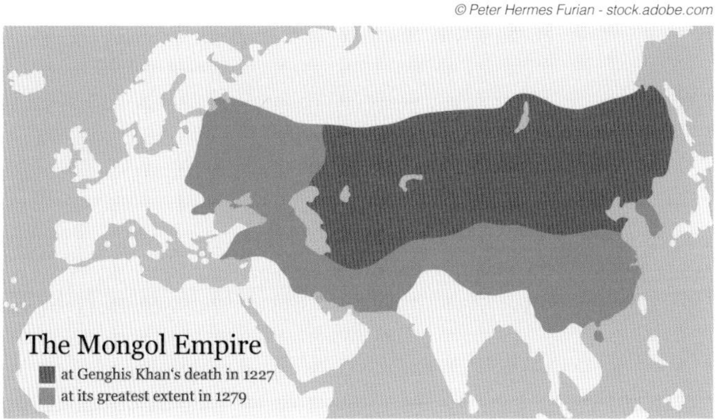


In September of 2006, while staying at the Intercontinental Hotel in Istanbul, I noticed that the nametag of the front desk staff read, Kublai. After greeting me with the obligatory, 'Welcome sir', I acknowledged his greeting and inquired about his name, the response came back as; 'I am Genghis. Oh, my father!'.

Checking into this response, I found that it was more of a joke. Although without a doubt the Mongolian Empire of Genghis Khan, (1155~1227) was expansive, however, the true great Khan is Kublai Khan. Genghis Khan is renowned for merging the Chinese continent consummating the Mongolian Empire. Genghis Khan's nephew, Kublai Khan was responsible for moving the capital Karakorum to the north, 'north' (北in Chinese character), 'capital' (京in Chinese character), becoming Peking (Beijing) of today.

Although written records do not exist, it is said that in 1162 Genghis Khan was born in the northern region of Mongol as the first son to father Yesügei and his second wife. His birthname was Temujin. When Temujin was 9 years old, his father moved him to the home of Temujin's new wife. However, when his father was invited to a festival of another tribe, he was poisoned. Temujin immediately returned home to lay claim to his father's position as chief of the tribe, but the tribe refused, due to his youth. Oppositely the tribe decided to banish him,

テムジン、9歳の折、10歳のボルテ・カーツン（Borte Khatun）と婚約。17歳で結婚、彼女が最初の妻である。妻の持参金を使ってオング・カーン（Ong Khan）と同盟を結んだ。彼はテムジンの父親とは血のつながる兄弟である。そしてネストリヤ派キリスト教徒（Nestorian Christian）でもある。

しかし、好事魔多し。マーキツ部族（Merkits）に襲われ、男は馬で逃げた。逃げ遅れたボルテは8カ月の間、略奪され・凌辱されて、奪い返したときには身ごもっていた。生まれたのは男児で、名はジョチ（Jochi）。テムジンは自身の子として扱ったが、テムジンにとっては辛いことであった。ただ人は、このような苦しみの中で自らを大きくしていくのである。

ジンギス汗（当時テムジン）は、これを機に中原の覇を目指すことを決意したという。ゴールデン・ホルデ（Golden Horde）と呼ばれたモンゴル帝国軍の総司令官としてオスマン帝国を築き上げたジョチは、国母と尊敬されたジンギス汗の妻の実子でもあり、ジョチ・カーン（Jochi Khan）となった。同時に父のジンギス汗が中原の覇者となるべく先頭に立って戦闘に明け暮れたのである。そして父ジンギス汗に北方を任されて現在のモスクワを有力な地方都市として開発した。

ジンギス汗は、中国を征服するに及んだが、彼の中国支配は北方、すなわち万里の長城の北側、北京辺りまでであった。しかし彼の未来を見る目の確かさ・戦に対する知恵・実行は、第6話で述べたアレキサンダー大王とその父親の戦略と同じである、時は違っても。騎馬隊によるスピード・アップなど。

中国全土を併合したのは、ジンギス汗の甥になるフビライ汗である。1271年には国名をモンゴル（Mongolia）から中国風の元と改めた。マルコ・ポーロと会い、日本が黄金の国と聞き、日本を襲撃した元寇は有名な話である。この元も、漢民族の明に敗れモンゴル高原に去り（1368年）、北元となった。ジンギス汗の誕生から206年後の元王朝の終焉である。

forcing him to experience poverty and hardship. It was during this period, that an argument erupted over the share of a successful hunt, resulting in Temujin killing his step brother. For this he was imprisoned for 5 years.

Temujin, was 9 years old when he was engaged to Borte, who was 10 years old at the time. At the age of 17, they were married, and she became his first wife. Using his wife's dowry, he made an alliance with Ong Khan, a blood brother of Temujin's father. He was also a Nestorian Christian.

However, clouds lurk near the sunshine. Attacked by Merkits, the man was forced to flee on horseback. Borte, who was late in fleeing, was abducted, abused and held captive for 8 months, and when she was rescued by Temujin, she was pregnant. A boy was born, and was named Jochi. Although Temujin raised the child as his own, it was a painful reminder for Temujin. People often say, it is within experiencing these hardships that an individual makes himself larger.

It was through these events that, Genghis Khan (at the time Temujin), determined to aim for the domination of Zhong-yuan. As commander of the Mongolian Imperial Army, also known as the Golden Horde, establishing the Ottoman Empire was Jochi, later becoming Jochi Khan, who was the son of Genghis Khan's wife, revered and respected, as the mother of the nation. At the same time, he was tirelessly combatting in the front lines to ensure that his father, Genghis Khan would become the dominator of Zhong-yuan. In time, Genghis Khan entrusted him with the norther territory, which he developed into a powerful northern capital city, currently known as Moscow.

Although Genghis Khan endeavored to conquer China, in reality, the territory he conquered was the northern region, specifically, was the northern side of the Great Wall, the area of Beijing. However, the accuracy of his vision of the future, his knowledge toward combat and implementation is; as noted in Narrative 6, although the period in which they fought differs, is strategically the same as that of Alexander the Great, and that of his father's. Such as the acceleration of speed in combat with the utilization of a calvary, etc.

The unification of the entirety of China was made by his nephew, Kublai Khan. In 1271 he altered the nation's name from Mongolia to the Chinese 'Yuan'. Meeting with Marco Polo, hearing that Japan was a land of gold, made the decision to invade Japan, which became the famous Mongol invasion. This Yuan, after being defeated by the Han Chinese' Ming, the Mongols retreated to the northern plains of Mongol (1368) which became North Yuan. 206 years after the birth of Genghis Khan, became the end of the Yuan Dynasty.

## 第16話

初出：2020年6月22日

# コロナで苦境の自動車業界で“今”必要な大物——リー・アイアコッカ

© Science Source/amanaimages

*Lee Iacocca*
リー・アイアコッカ

懐かしい名前だ。ちょうど筆者がミシガン州カラマズー市のアップジョン社に赴任した頃（1986年）の米国自動車業界、いや米国産業界のカリスマ経営者であった方である。人に歴史あり（東京12チャンネル、1968年〜1981年）、波乱万丈の人生だった。

よく、“怒るな—威張るな—のんびり—負けるな”と言われますが、アイアコッカ氏（Lee Iacocca、1924年〜2019年）は正反対で“怒る—威張る—急ぐ—勝つ”が基本の人だったような気がする。メンタルには疲れるライフスタイルですね。本当は孤独で寂しかったかもしれない。

さてアイアコッカ氏は、名前の通りイタリア系の在米2世である。誕生時の名前はリド・アンソニー・アイアコッカ（Lido Anthony Iacocca）であるが、通称リー・アイアコッカである。両親はペンシルヴァニア（Pennsylvania）でレストラン・Yocco's Hot Dogsのオーナーだった。新婚旅行で行ったヴェニスのリド（Lido）地域が印象に残り、息子にリド（Lido）と名付けたという。Lidoが愛称Leeになったということであろう。

アイアコッカ氏は1942年、ハイスクールを優秀な成績（honors）で卒業。リーハイ（Lehigh）大学で工学エンジニアリングを専攻している。そして奨学金を得て、プリンストン大学の専科（Electives）に入り政治

Narrative16

# The Automotive Industry in the Corona Predicament, "Now" Needs Heavyweight Lee  Iacocca (passed away last year)

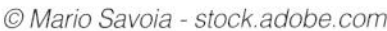

A memorable name. It just so happened that it was during the time I was employed by Upjohn, which was located in Kalamazoo, Michigan (1986), Lee Iacocca, not limited to the America's automotive industry, but America's industry sector, was a charismatic business executive. In a television program 'History within an Individual' (Tokyo 12 Channel, 1968~1981), introduced his turbulent and eventful life.

It is often said, "Don't get angry, don't brag, take it slow and don't lose", however I think Mr. Iacocca was the absolute opposite, an individual who was fundamentally; "Angry, brags, in a rush, and wins". A lifestyle that is completely exhausting mentally. In a likelihood, he was secluded and experienced loneliness.

Mr. Iacocca (1924~2019), as evident in the name, is 2nd generation Italian American. Although at birth, he was christened Lido Anthony Iacocca, he was commonly known as Lee Iacocca. His parents were the owners of restaurant Yocco's Hot Dogs located in Pennsylvania. On their honeymoon his parent's visited Venice's Lido district, which had left a strong impression upon them, thus they decided to name their son Lido. Lee most likely becoming a nickname for Lido.

Mr. Iacocca, in 1942, graduated from high school with honors. He continued his education at Lehigh University, majoring in industrial engineering. Receiving a scholarship, he attended Princeton University where he took electives in politics and plastics. In 1946, he began

学・合成樹脂学を学ぶ。1946年、エンジニアとしてフォード（Ford Motor Company）に入社。フォードでは、有名なマスタング（Mustang）のエンジニアとして市場投入にかけがえのない役割を果たした。いささか鼻持ちならないやからとして煙たがられるが、セールスマネジャー次長として、社内の立ち位置を確立した。彼の“56－56”キャンペーンは有名だ。1956年の車に20％減のローンを組み、毎月56ドルを3年間支払うというものである。これが全国版となり出世街道まっしぐら、1970年にはフォード社の社長となる。時に46歳である。落ち目のクライスラー社（Chrysler Corporation）に三顧の礼で迎えられ、フォード社の人材を引きつれて入社。クライスラーといえば、ニューヨーク・マンハッタンのクライスラービル（The Art Deco Chrysler Building）が人目を惹く。しかし、再建には、お金が要る。1979年、彼は下院（US Congress）に資金調達を訴え、うまい具合にローンの裏付けを得た。条件として人員整理・不採算部門の切り捨てなどを試み、再建に乗りだした。1987年、かの有名ブランドとなったジープ（Jeep Grand Cherokee）のAMC（アメリカン・モーターズ）を買収。1993年、モデル発表と同時にクライスラーを退任した。その後、カーク・カーコリアン（Kirk Kerkorian）の敵対的買収に絡んだりした。一時期成功かと思われた時もあったが、クライスラーの再建は成功しなかった。結局、2014年1月、イタリアのフィアット社が買収。フィアット・クライスラー・オートモービルス（Fiat Chrysler Automobiles）として、ゼネラルモーターズ（GM）、フォードと並んで米国自動車業界の3大メーカーとなっている。

晩年は、パーキンソン病に冒されたというが、素晴らしい人生を送り、一時大統領候補とまで噂された偉人であった。

湖北台の夕日

「素心湖北台有志の会メンバーズ」

his career in the Fords Motor Company as an engineer. At Ford, he was instrumental in the design and marketing of the famous Mustang. Although an insufferable individual, making those around him uncomfortable, as assistant sales manager he established a solid position within the corporation. His famous "56 for 56" campaign gained national recognition. This campaign offered loans on 1956 model cars with a 20% down payment and monthly payments of 56 dollars for 3 years. This campaign went national, and he went on to quickly go up the ranks, in 1970 he was appointed president of Ford Motor Company. At the time, he was 46 years old. The Chrysler Corporation, which was doing very badly, courted Mr. Iacocca, who along with other employees of Ford, joined Chrysler. Speaking of Chrysler, the Art Deco Chrysler Building in Manhattan, New York attracts attention. However, rebuilding costs money. In 1979, Mr. Iacocca approached the U.S. Congress and successfully won a loan guarantee. Accepting all the necessary in obtaining this loan, such as; the reduction of employees and abandoning divisions that are losing money, he went into rebuilding the corporation. In 1987, acquiring the famous Jeep brand (Jeep Grand Cherokee) through the acquisition of AMC (American Motors) was made. In 1993, the year in which the Grand Cherokee was released, he retired. After retiring, he assisted Kirk Kerkorian's hostile takeover. Although for a period it looked as though that Chrysler would succeed, ultimately efforts to rebuild it was unsuccessful. At the end, in January of 2014, Chrysler was acquired by Italy's Fiat. Now known as Fiat Chrysler Automobiles, alongside General Motors (GM) and Ford, is one of America's top three automobile manufacturers.

In later years, although he suffered from Parkinson's disease, he had enjoyed a marvelous life, a great man who was once rumored to be a candidate for the U.S. presidency.

*To-be-planned-J—Tavern*

# 第17話

初出：2021年2月22日

# フランス皇帝ナポレオン・ボナパルト
## ——イングランド征服の夢を果たせなかった男

© Didier San Martin - stock.adobe.com

本論に入る前に、皇帝ナポレオン1世（Napoleon Bonaparte、1769年〜1821年）の白馬に跨る顔、特に目には、涙で潤んでいるような印象を持っていた。「オレ、頑張ってんだよ…」的な感じがしたのである。そして今回、詳しく彼の生涯を紐解くうちに、何となく理解できたような気になった。

彼の高祖父は、イタリアのコルシカ島（Corsica）の貧乏貴族であった。曾孫のナポレオン1世自身もイタリア生まれのイタリア人であった。9歳の時に、フランスに移住し神学校に入れられた。ところが神父様なんかに満足せず、奨学金を得て士官学校に転校している。この辺が、彼の「瓢箪から駒」、将来フランス皇帝になる運命の分岐点であった、9歳の時だ。そのころの仲間からは、イタリアなまり、チビ、フランス語が早くしゃべれないなどで、へこんでいた。まあー、「トレビの泉」で体くらいは洗っただろうが…。その代わりに、一人読書にのめりこんでいく。兵法も学び将来、百戦練磨の将軍・皇帝となる基本を、この頃（9歳児）、学んでいたのである。

そして、彼がフランス市民になったのはフランス軍将軍ナポレオンがイタリア国を征服統合した時である（1796年）。弱冠26歳である。ナポレオンが皇帝になったのは、35歳の時で（1804年5月）、ナポレオン1世

## Narrative 17

# France's Emperor Napoleon Bonaparte
## —— A Man Who Could Not Fulfill His Dream to Conquer England

Prior to going into the main subject of this narrative, my impression of Napoleon Bonaparte the first, (1769~1821) is of a man astride a white steed, with a tear wetting his eyes. "I, really tried." was the feeling that emitted. Then this time, while unraveling the details of his life, I felt that I was closer to understanding him.

His great grandfather was from a noble but impoverished family of Corsica Island of Italy. His great grandchild, Napoleon the first, was an Italian born in Italy. When Napoleon was 9 years old, he moved to France and entered a seminary. However, not content in becoming a priest, obtaining a scholarship he transferred to a military academy. This is where, at 9 years old, the unexpected becomes the turning point of the future emperor of France. During this time, he would be taunted by his peers with words such as; you have an Italian accent, shorty, you cannot speak French rapidly, depressing him. Well, perhaps an urge may have developed to wash the body in [the trivia fountain]. As a substitute, he sought refuge in reading books. Studying military strategy, at this time (a child of 9 years old), became the foundation of becoming a battle-hardened general and eventually emperor.

としてフランス国が認めたのだ。フランス人としてのフランス皇帝ナポレオン1世の誕生である。

ナポレオン（1世）が、51歳と8カ月余の生涯を閉じる臨終の時、ささやいた言葉が子供が出来ないので離婚した元愛妻、「ジョセフィーヌ」だったと言われる。実際は、彼女は彼より6歳年上だったと言われ、ナポレオンと出会う前の結婚で2人の子供に恵まれている。恋多き女性として有名だった彼女は、ナポレオンと結婚（1796年）しても何人かの恋人がおり、懐妊したら父親が確認できないから（DNA鑑定も無いし…）、それなりの対応を考えていたに違いない。ナポレオンは、一向に懐妊しないジョセフィーヌを見て、自分には種（しゅ）がないのかと自信を無くしていた。いやいや、ところがである。ナポレオンの愛人が懐妊し子供を授かったのである。これで自信を得たナポレオンは、懐妊できないという触れ込みで、ジョセフィーヌと離婚。

そして、さすがフランス皇帝ナポレオン、神聖ローマ帝国の主宰である名門中の名門オーストリアのハプスブルグ家（Haus Hapsburg）のマリー・ルイース（Marie Louise）と再婚し、男の子が誕生。ナポレオン2世となる。父ナポレオン1世が亡くなると、静かな余生を送ったと言われる。

この辺で、表題に戻りたい。イタリア併合からヨーロッパ大陸は自分の庭みたいなもので、庭での戦争ごっこなら連戦連勝があたり前である。…前田のクラッカーだ。それでも大将軍・大皇帝なのに、勝てない地域があった。経験したことのない地域：海と凍土である。ロマノフ王朝のツァーに敗れて、（映画で見た）雪が降る中をソリに引かれて行くナポレオンの威厳を保とうと口をキリッと結んだ表情は忘れられない。

そして、英国国教の創設をはじめ、ヨーロッパからの独立を国是としてきた英国。英国の文化のレベルの高さに憧れていたナポレオンにとっては、その英国を併合することが長年の夢であった。屈強なフランス人を率いて、何度か英国海軍と戦ったが、海戦のプロフェッショナル、ネルソン総督には歯が立たなかった。

Napoleon only became a French citizen when, as a general of the French army, he conquered Italy and unified it with France (1796). He was only 26 years old at the time. Napoleon became the emperor when he was 35 years old (May, 1804), becoming Napoleon the First, and rule over France. The was when, as a Frenchman, Napoleon the First, emperor of France was born.

It is said that when Napoleon (the First) on his deathbed, in the midst of ending his life at 51 years and 8 months, the last word he uttered was the name of the woman that he divorced due to her inability to bear his children, [Josephine]. In fact, it is said that she was 6 years older than he was, ad when she met Napoleon, she had 2 children from her prior marriage. Famous for having numerous affairs, she continued having several lovers after her marriage (1796) with Napoleon, if she was to become pregnant there would be no means to confirm who the father of the child was, (DNA testing was not available), I am confident that certainly methods were considered to deal with such circumstances. Napoleon, upon seeing that Josephine was showing no signs of becoming pregnant, doubted his that perhaps he was to blame, loosing confidence. No, no, what do you know. Napoleon's lover became pregnant. Regaining confidence, Napoleon, accusing Josephine of not being able to become pregnant, divorced her.

Then, worthy of a French emperor, Napoleon, remarried Marie Louise, from the famed House of Hapsburg, which had held the throne of the Holy Roman Empire for centuries, a son was born, becoming Napoleon II. It is said that following the death of his father, Napoleon the First, lived his life quietly.

Let us return to the entitled. After the annexation of Italy, the European continent became similar to his own backyard, battles within this backyard would certainly result in victorious results. The Maeda Cracker. Although he was the feared and accomplished general, as well as, emperor, there was a territory that he could not conquer. A territory that was unexperienced: which was the sea and frozen ground. Defeated by the Romanov dynasty tour, (I have seen it in a movie) an unforgettable image of the dignified Napoleon being pulled by a sleigh through the snow.

Beginning with establishing the borders of the United Kingdom, and its national policy to ensure its independence from Europe. For Napoleon, who had been impressed by the height of England's culture, had an enduring dream to annex England. Leading the strong French, he repeated engaged with the British navy, however, he was no match for the naval warfare professional Viscount Nelson

Globalization
つれづれに人(ひと)を敬う

# 第3章
## 活動中の人々

Globalization

# Respecting People As the Time is Passing

# Article 3

## Active the Greats

# 第18話

初出：2019年12月23日

# 林　諄――日本医療経営実践協会を創立

日本医療企画の林諄社長との出会いに触れるとき、忘れられない人が二人いる。一人は東京女子医科大学の故・櫻井靖久名誉教授（2011年没）である。私が米国アップジョン（Upjohn and Company）の日本法人の代表者兼米国本社VPの時、アップジョンアウォード選考委員になっていただいてからの付き合いである（1987年）。もう一人が、田辺製薬の故・加藤義男さん（2006年没）である。私が米国E.リリー社の日本支社にいたころ、櫻井先生の主宰する会で講演を頼まれ、その会場で加藤さんが林社長を私に紹介してくれたというのが、林社長との出会いの経緯である。そして林社長を通して、日本医療企画との絆ができ、日本医療経営実践協会で意見を述べる機会があるといった次第でもある。加藤さんは、田辺製薬でスモン（SMON：整腸剤キノホルムによる被害）の対策を担当し、法務の勉強を徹底的にして、実践家としては弁護士以上の知識を持った人であった。

林社長は一言でいうと、Serious and Shyな人である。Seriousすなわち“真面目・強い正義感”があり、しかも“シャイ”な人間臭い男である。1939年、石川県鹿島郡鳥屋町（現中能登町）に生まれ、生家は兼業農家であったが、当時の地元の名家である。父親は炭火焼き木炭のコンロを

Narrative 18

# Jun Hayashi —— Founder of the Japan Medical Management Practice Association

To introduce how I met President Jun Hayashi of Japan Medical Planning, there are two individuals I cannot forget. One is the late (deceased,2011) Yasuhisa Sakurai, professor emeritus of Tokyo Women's Medical University's. Our relationship started, when I was the Japan representative and VP of their U.S. headquarters of the American pharmaceutical corporation, Upjohn and Company, and he graciously undertook the task of becoming a member of the nomination committee for the Upjohn Award (1987). The other individual is the late (deceased, 2006), Mr. Yoshio Kato of Tanabe Seiyaku Co., Ltd. It was through President Hayashi, that I established a network with Japan Medical Planning, which led to the opportunity in expressing my opinions within the Japan Medical Management Practice Association. Mr. Kato at Tanabe Seiyaku, was responsible for countermeasures toward damages related to (SMON: intestinal chinoform) to do so, he studied law so extensively, that he accumulated knowledge, in this respect, that surpasses a professional lawyer.

In describing President Hayashi, in short, he is a serious and shy individual. When referring to serious, it reflects his "honestly and a strong sense of justice", however, "shy" reflects his down-to-earth, aspects. Born in 1939 in Toriya Machi (currently Nakanoto Machi), Kashima Gun, Ishikawa Prefecture, although his family were farmers with side jobs, during this period, were a regional distinguished family. His father was the owner of a company which made charcoal burning cookers, (Isolite Insulating Products Co., Ltd.). Recently, their products are those that are seeing a revival in the popularity of charcoal burning heating products. It seems that during his childhood, he was a baseball boy and leader of the gang. It is easy to assume that he his teachers were fond of him. A similarity with Russia's Gorbachev's childhood days. Known for his continued love of baseball, as manager of a baseball team of the pharmaceuti-

作った経営者(イソライト工業)だった。最近、盛んになって来た暖房の炭火焼き木炭である。どうも小さい時は、野球小僧でガキ大将だったらしい。先生には、可愛がられたのではないか。ゴルバチョフ(ロシア)の少年時代に似ている。野球部は今でも捨てがたく、監督として業界では独り勝ち。県立神戸商科大学(現兵庫県立大学)を経て、兵庫新聞社からサンケイ新聞の記者になった。持前の正義感が頭をもたげ、押しの一手で権威筋からは、煙たがられたという。この押しの一手で、ミス神戸を娶った辺りは捨て置けない。塞翁が馬だね、連れ帰ったのは馬ではなくて美女だけど。

一時期政界に興味を持った時期があったが、これはやめてよかった。政治家はウソを言っても許される日本の政界では、その正義感の強さから腹が立ってヒックリかねない。

真面目で正義感があるから、いろいろな事業を手掛けて失敗をしている。が、本業である日本医療企画の経営は順調である故にいろんなことにチャレンジできるのであろう。その一つが日本医療経営実践協会の創立である(2010年)。厳格な試験をもとに、医療経営士3級、2級そして1級の資格認定を行っている。現在、3級(約1万人)、2級(約1400人)そして1級(64人)の医療経営士が誕生し、日本の医療の生産性向上に向けて機能・実践している。これはすごいことである。もちろん、松村役員をはじめ協会スタッフや、吉原代表をはじめ理事の方々、須田さん、清水さんといった月例会の方々、濃沼先生を中心とする試験委員の皆さまの活躍もあっての話である。

さて、林社長の人間をもう少し語りたい。月例役員会や理事会では、我慢してジーと聞いている。時々、気にするように意見を言うのがシャイで人間臭い。よく行く寿司屋では、下戸の私に付き合ってノン・アルコール・ビールを飲んでくれる。二人とも話は好きなので、時間を忘れる。2020年、日本医療企画が40周年、実践協会が10周年を迎えるという。よき友に、乾杯!

calindustry, the team was a constant winner. After graduating the Kobe University of Commerce (the now, Hyogo University), he became a journalist for the Hyogo Shimbun and later the Sankei Shimbun (newspaper). His strong sense of justice was his driving force, resulting in those of authority to become wary of him. This driving force also enabled him to win over Miss Hyogo. Fortune comes in mysterious ways; in his case it was a beautiful lady.

There was a period in which he held an interest toward the politics, however, it was in his favor that he terminated furthering this interest. Within Japanese politics, politicians get away with lying, from his strong sense of justice, it is highly predictable that he would become extremely angry as well as astonished.

It is due to his sense of honesty and justice that the many business projects he initiated met with failure. Yet, it is likely that the favorable progress of his main business, Japan Medical Planning, is the foundation that enables him to proceed in getting involved with other challenges. One of which is the Japan Medical Management Practice Association, established in 2010. The Association, through stringent examinations, provide individuals with 3rd, 2nd, or 1st level health manager qualifications. Currently, as a result there are new health managers; 3rd level (approximately, 10,000 individuals), 2nd level (an estimated 1,400 individuals), and 1st level (64 individuals), which through their functions and practices, are contributing to the productivity of Japan's health care. Needless to say, these impressive results are only possible with the efforts made by, executives such as Mr. Matsumura, as well as the Association's staff, representative Mr. Yoshiwara, directors such as Mr. Suda, Mr. Shimizu, who are members of the monthly meetings, and the examination committee led by Professor Koinuma.

I would like to touch a little upon President Hayashi as a human being. At the monthly executives meeting or director's meetings, in silence he patiently listens. At intervals, he puts forward his personal opinion with care, reflecting his down-to-earth, shyness. At the sushi restaurant that he frequented, taking into account that I cannot drink, he would drink non-alcohol beer. Both of us enjoy talking, forgetting the time passing. 2020 marks the 40th anniversary of the Japan Medical Planning, and the 10th anniversary of the Japan Medical Management Practice Association. I toast a dear friend!

## 第19話

初出：2018年10月8日

# 北海道のカリスマ二人 ——寶金清博・田中繁道

カリスマ(Charisma)という言葉はよく聞く。"彼はまさにカリスマだよ"などなど。どうもカリスマには条件がありそうである。第1に、「強烈な自信(Strong self－confidence)」である。自信過剰ではない。第2に、「その強烈な自信を表に出さない静けさ(Calm)」である。そして強烈な自信に基づく「タイムリーな決断(Timely decision)」である。

たまたま、筆者が代表理事代行を務めている日本医療経営実践協会の「変革期の病院経営——次世代病院リーダーのための基礎力向上セミナー」を、2018年6月30日にTKP札幌駅カンファレンスセンターにて、北海道大学病院（寶金清博病院長）および札幌医科大学附属病院（土橋和文病院長）と共催した。その時、総合司会をお願いしたのが寶金先生であった。道内各地の病院、医療関係施設から200人近くの方々が参画し、活発な意見の交換がなされた。これは、寶金先生と土橋先生の呼びかけによるものであった。寶金先生による基調講演「病院のガバナンス」は、飾らない落ち着きの中、思いがけないスライド（サッカーワールドカップのスナップショットな

## Narrative 19

# The Charismatic Two Soshin Consulting

*Secretaries* ／秘書

長内先生

We often hear the word charisma. For instance, the phrase, "He possesses charisma". However, it seems that there are certain requirements regarding charisma. First, one must possess an extremely strong sense of self-confidence. This is not to be mistaken with overconfidence. Secondly, the capability of veiling the strong self-confidence and sustaining an overall calmness. Thirdly, the capability to make crucial and timely decisions based upon the strong self-confidence.

It just so happens that I hold the position of Acting Representative Director of the Japan Medical Management Practice Association. On June 30th, 2018, the Association held a seminar entitled, [Hospital Management in The Period of Change—Advancing Basic Capabilities of the Next Generation] at TKP Sapporo Station Conference Center in co-sponsorship with Director, Kiyohiro Hokin of Hokkaido University Hospital, and Director, Kazufumi Tsuchihashi of Sapporo Medical University. We requested the assistance of Dr. Hokin as Master of Ceremonies. There were close to 200 participants, representing hospitals and related medical institutions from areas within Hokkaido, who partook in active discussions. This seminar was the result of Drs. Hokin and Tsuchibashi call. Within Dr. Hokin's keynote speech, [Hospital Governance] which was given with casual calmness, unforeseen slides were at intervals includ-

ど）を時折織り交ぜながら、ガバナンス（Governance）と管理（Administration）の違い：前者はトップダウンであり後者はボトムアップである——を示しつつ、両者を使い分けながら病院運営を行っている、とさりげなく述べられた。お見事！

また、千葉大の井上貴裕特任教授の再三にわたる例を示しながらの「投資は最後は負債になる」は、素晴らしい教訓であった。

さらに渓仁会グループ最高責任者兼渓仁会理事長の田中繁道氏による「病院経営改革を成功に導くリーダーシップと組織改革」と、同じグループの田中いずみ看護部長の「病院経営を成功に導く看護部門の実践マネジメント」も圧巻であった。このグループの17年度のキャッシュフローは、約440億円であったという。これは道内国立大学の約2倍であり、道内トップである。これこそ田中グループ長の手腕であり、前述のトップダウンとボトムアップの使い分けの見事な実践でもある。

こうして筆者は、このお二人、寳金清博氏と田中繁道氏を北海道のカリスマと呼びたい。

さて筆者が仕えてきた直接の上司の中に、カリスマはいたであろうか。まず三菱時代（三菱油化、医薬部門）、上司にはカリスマには程遠い人ばかりだった。当時三菱化成に在籍していた経済同友会代表幹事の小林喜光氏は、大学院はイスラエルという若いころの足跡からも国際人であり、笑顔を絶やさず他人（ひと）の話もよく聞く。TVでの発言もメリハリはっきり、この人はまさにカリスマである。米国アップジョン時代では、テッド・クーパー（Ted Cooper）CEOはカリスマだった。いつも笑顔で小柄であるが、時に雷が落ちると皆震え上がっていた。なぜか筆者は、君はグローバル人間だからと、同僚がうらやむほどにかわいがってもらった。E.リリー時代では、入社の役員面接（当時エクゼクティブVP、1994年）の時から気が合っていまだに友人である有機化学出身のCEO（17年退任）であったジョン・レックライター（John Lechleiter）は、部下への評価でプラス（＋）とマイナス（－）の明確な、実に気持ちの良い公平なカリスマだった。

ed within his presentation (e.g. snapshots of the soccer World Cup), explained the difference between governance and administration; while reflecting that for former is applied from the top-down, the later from the bottom-up, he effortlessly demonstrated how the utilization of both were applied in hospital management. Fantastic!

In addition, Dr. Hokin, repeatedly introduced examples of Specially Appointed Professor, Takahiro Inoue of Chiba University concept of [Investments ultimately lead to burden] reflecting an extremely beneficial lesson.

Also, Chief Executive and Director of Keijin Kai Group, Mr. Shigemichi Tanaka, spoke on [Leadership and Organizational Reform Leading to Successful Hospital Management Reform] and Ms. Izumi Tanaka, Nursing Director of the same group spoke on [Successful Hospital Management Reform thru Established Management of the Nursing Division] were indeed highlights. It is said that the Group's 2017 cashflow was roughly 44 billion yen (0.4 billion U.S. dollars). This figure is roughly double that of Hokkaido's National University hospitals and is top within Hokkaido. Unmistakably the result of Group Director Tanaka's capability, as well as a remarkable example of the aforementioned, application of both top-down and bottom-up practices in hospital management.

This is why I refer to these two gentlemen; Dr. Kiyohiro Hokin and Mr. Shigemichi Tanaka as charismatic figures.

Here, I would like to reflect as to whether there was a charismatic figure among the direct superiors I worked under. To start with, the period when I was with Mitsubishi, (Medical Division of Mitsubishi Yuka K.K.), my superiors were far from being charismatic. During that time, Mr. Yoshimitsu Kobayashi, the current Chairman of the Japan Association of Corporate Executives, was employed by Mitsubishi Chemical Corp. Attending graduate school in Israel, in his youth his footprints reflected that he was an international minded individual, always showing a smile, with the capability to truly listen to what people say. On occasions where he appears in televised programs, his comments are clear and to the point, he possesses charisma. During my years with the U.S. pharmaceutical firm Upjohn, the CEO, Mr. Ted Cooper was charismatic. Although always smiling and small in stature, when he roared, everyone trembled. However, for some reason, to my colleagues' envy, he took great care of me, often saying 'You are global individual.' My years with Eli Lilly, an individual who I hit it off with from the time of my executive interview session, (at the time; 1994 Executive VP), and who is still a dear friend, is John Lechleiter. His background is in Organic Chemistry, and was later appointed CEO, retiring in 2017. When evaluating the performance of his subordinates, he utilized a clear plus and minus system, a truly fair and refreshing charismatic individual.

第20話　　初出：2018年11月12日

# 国境なき医師団／Médecins Sans Frontières

© alamy/amanaimages

1999年10月10日にノーベル平和賞を受賞した"国境なき医師団"はグローバルにはMédecins Sans Frontières(MSF)とフランス語で表記される。それは、民間・非営利の立場で医療・人道援助活動を行う国際団体として、フランスで設立されたからである。時に1971年。1992年には日本オフィスもできている。

ノーベル平和賞受賞時のグローバルプレジデントであったジェームスJ. オルビンスキー(James Jude Orbinski、1960年～)は、英国生まれの医師である。医師としてのトレーニングはカナダで受けている。生理学をトレント大学(Trent University、Montreal)で学び、医学をマックマスター大学(McMaster University、Hamilton)で学び医師となった。昨年(2017年)には、カナダ・トロントのヨーク大学(York University)のグローバル医療研究ダーダレー研究所(Dahdaleh)の初代所長(Inaugural Director)に就任している。

彼のこのような活動の原点は、何だったのだろうか。思い立ったからといっても、急にできるものでもない。ジェームス少年は、1967年に両親とともにモントリオールの土を踏んだ。その時、出会ったカナダ警察の制服：真っ赤なジャケットに革製のブーツを纏った2人の警察官に魅せられ、カナダのために尽くしたいと誓ったという。The Mounties(マウンテーズ)と呼ばれる、カナダ警官のその偉丈夫さに圧

## Narrative 20

# Médecins Sans Frontières

© 朝日新聞社／アマナイメージズ

国境なき医師団(MSF)
日本前会長 加藤寛幸

On October 10, 1999 winners of the Nobel Peace Prize was the global health professionals organization Médecins Sans Frontières(MSF)widely known in Japan as 'Physicians without Boarders'. The organization operates on a private and non-profit basis providing humanitarian efforts. This organization was established in France in 1971, thus the French name, and has opened an office in Japan in 1992.

Accepting the Nobel Peace Prize was Global President, James Jude Orbinski (1960~), a physician who was born in England. Receiving his training as a physician in Canada, educated in phycology at Trent University of Montreal, a medical degree from McMaster University, Hamilton. In 2017, Dr. Orbinski his became the inaugural director of the Dahdaleh Institute of Global Health Research at York University in Toronto, Canada.

What was it that motivated him to become so deeply involved with humanitarian efforts? It is not something that one just thinks of doing one day. In 1967, the young James arrived with his parent in Montreal. Upon seeing two members of the Canadian police force in their uniform of a bright red jacket and leather boots, he became captivated, and swore to contribute to Canada. It is most likely that he was overwhelmed by the strength The Mounties, as the Canadian police force is called, embodied. Perhaps this encounter eventually lead to his joining MSF.

I would now like to touch upon the organization's activities in Japan. The current Director is Dr. Hiroyuki Kato. In the September 18th, 2018 evening edition of Nihon Keizai Shimbun (newspaper), within the column 'Ningen Hakken', provides in-depth details. I suggest that the article be read. Prior to joining MSF his life was quite momentous. Dr. Kato was raised in a single-parent home by his mother. The memories of loneliness when he was a small

倒されたのであろう。そして、それが長じてMSFに入ることにもつながったのであろう。

さて、この辺で国境なき医師団日本の活動について触れたい。会長(当時)は加藤寛幸氏である。日本経済新聞夕刊の人間発見(2018年9月18日からの一週間)に詳しい。一読をおすすめしたい。MSFに入る前がすでに波乱万丈である。加藤さんは母子家庭に育った。寂しかった幼い頃の思いから、今でも困った他人(ひと)がいれば駆け付けたいという思いに駆られるという。最初北海道大学理学部に入ったが、人助けのできる医学部に入りなおそうとして、島根医科大学医学部(1986年)に入学している。アルバイトをしながら苦学。6年生となり進路に悩んでいた時期に親友に連れられて行ったプロテスタントの教会で役職(長老)の女性に出会いある言葉を聞き、それが人生の指針になったという。“人の嫌がることをしなさい”と。

MSFのTV広告を見て興味を持ったが、MSFに正式に入団するのに、10年かかったという。面接で2回も落ちたという。1度目は語学力不足、2度目は臨床スキル不足が理由だった。ここがMSFの凄いところで、現地で生かせる医学の知識と体験を身につけなくてはならないのである。志だけでは通用しない世界である。世の中一生懸命生きている人々にとっては、それぞれの職業は皆厳しいが、他人のためになっているのである。

そして加藤さんは、今までに9回も国内外の被災地に派遣されているという。ご自身とご家族のご健勝を心からお祈りしたい。

また、日経新聞(2018年10月29日)で日本副会長の吉野美幸医師(外科医)の活動も知ることができた。益々のご活躍とご自愛をお祈りしたい。またMSFの仕事は真のチーム医療である。シエラレオネのエボラ治療センターで活躍された大滝潤子看護師にも心からの声援をおくりたい。シエラレオネ共和国は西アフリカの西部、大西洋に位置する共和制国家で、イギリス連邦加盟国である。

child has instilled the need to rush to help those in need. Although originally admitted to the School of Science, of Hokkaido University, he re-took studies and examinations to pursue medicine that would enable him to be of help to others, enrolling into Shimane Medical University in 1986. Working his way through school with part-time jobs. In his 6th year, when he was seriously thinking about what career path to take, a friend took him to a Protestant church where he met an elder of the church, who said "Do what others would not like to do." What she had said has become his beacon in life.

Although original interest toward MSF was through the organization's television advertisement, to officially be accepted into MSF took 10 years. He had failed at two interview sessions. The first was due to his lack in English language capabilities, the second was due to insufficient clinical skills. This is where MSF is outstanding, they require their members to possess medical knowledge and experience that can be utilized in their efforts on site. It is a world in which determination alone will suffice. People all around the world are concentrated and striving to live, and in doing so, they may find that their respective occupations are hard and difficult, however, at the end of the day, they are benefiting others.

Dr. Kato has, to date, been assigned 9 times to foreign and domestic stricken areas. I sincerely pray for his and his family's continued wellbeing.

In addition, an article of the October 29, 2018, Nihon Keizai Shimbun (newspaper), I was able to learn of the activities of the organization's Vice Director, Dr. Yukimi Yoshino (surgeon). To which I will pray for her progressive efforts. MSF's activities represent true team medicine. I would like to send like to send my heart-felt support to Ms. Junko Otaki who is a nurse at the Sierra Leone Ebola Treatment Center. The Republic of Sierra Leone is located on the southwest Atlantic coast of Africa, and has an uninterrupted democratic government. Formerly a British colony, it was granted its independence in 1961.

# 第21話

初出：2019年1月28日

# 鄧小平と習近平

© ZUMA Press/amanaimages

*Deng Xiaoping*
鄧小平（1904～1997）

最近の中国関係ニュースでは、かつての最高実力者鄧小平と現国家主席の習近平を比較する記事を内外とも多く見る、中国経済の先行きが怪しくなってから。習近平は、ご存じのごとく聡明で、死んだふりをよくやる人でもある。一帯一路をぶち上げ、2017年から2018年にかけて、汚職追及の親友、王岐山を片腕として異例の待遇（年齢越を免除）で遇し、自らも核心（コア）の称号を得、任期制限を撤廃する法改正により事実上の終身国家主席（President in Life）となったころに比べると最近ちょっと湿りがち。江沢民や胡錦濤が上海をそぞろ歩いてみたり、急進派の学生が一帯一路のビラを焼いてみたりと…。その辺は、習近平は百も承知で、筆者はあんまり心配してないが。

鄧小平と習近平。鄧小平は1978年の12月、共産党第11期三中全会（国会に相当）において毛沢東と四人組の文化大革命を批判し、改革路線をぶち上げパラマウント・リーダー（最高指導者）として激賞された。ご承知のごとく深圳を中心とする改革路線は成功し、今日の中国経済の発展のルート（root／根）となった。その時、鄧小平路線の説明隊の中心を務めたのが、何と習近平の父親・習仲勲であったという。人の巡り合わせは不思議であるが、筆者は何かの必然があると信じている。

文化大革命で辛酸を何度もなめさせられ、都度旧友の周恩来に目をか

## Narrative 21

# Deng Xiaoping and Xi Jinping

© Sipa Press/amanaimages

*Xí Jìnpíng*
習近平（1953 ～）

In recent China related news, following the uncertainty of China's economy, there is an abundance of domestic and international articles, that compare former influential Chinese leader, Deng Xiaoping, and the current President of China, Xi Jinping. Xi Jinping, as everyone is aware, intelligent, and is known to frequently play dead. Introducing the One Belt One Road Initiative, from 2017 to 2018 his close friend and corruption investigator, Wang Qishan as his other arm, received exceptional treatment with the removal of the term limits for the presidency, effectively becoming President for Life, and succeeding in becoming the core of centralized power, in comparison to these events, recently his power has slightly dampened. Jiang Zamin and Hu Jintao can be seen taking walks around Shanghai, radical faction students are burning One Belt One Road flyers. Xi Jinping is well aware of these incidents, I am not that worried.

Deng Xiaoping and Xi Jinping. On December, 1978, Deng Xiaoping at the 11th Third Plenum criticized Mao Zedong and the Gang of Four's Cultural Revolution, through introducing reforms he was praised and was awarded the title Paramount Leader of the People's Republic of China. As it is widely known, the success of economic reforms centralized in Shenzhen, is the root of today's Chinese economic developments. At that time, as a member of the explanation corps of Den Xiaoping's strategy was Xi Jinping's father, Xi Zhongxun. It is strange how the interaction of individuals can be, I cannot help but feel that this was inevitable.

Suffering repeated hardships through the Cultural Revolution, each time his old friend, Zhou Enlai would keep an eye on him, in comparison to the reinstated Deng Xiaoping challenging of Mao Zedong, Xi Jinping used the word 'invoke' when referring to Mao Zedong. What was his intentions? Perhaps he was trying to convey his inability to surpass Mao Ze-

けられ、よみがえった鄧小平の毛沢東へのチャレンジに比し、習近平は、毛沢東に対してinvoke(頼りにしています)という言葉を使ったのである。意図は何か。毛沢東にはかないません、鄧小平の改革路線はわたくしの父親がやりましたのでと、毛沢東と鄧小平の両者を持ち上げてみせたのではないかと思う。

そこで、待った！と声を上げたのが、米国在住の鄧小平の息子、鄧朴方である。「しかし、最近の習氏は、核心の称号と終身国家主席になってから、計画経済(価格統制など)を進めておる気配がする。わが親父(おやじ)である鄧小平が始めた市場経済(Marketisation　国営企業を民間の手法で統治する)を進めるべきではないのか」という(「フィナンシャル・タイムズ」2018年11月16日)。現実に、習氏が鄧小平時代のシステムを毛時代に戻す案件が見られるようになっている。どうしたことか。いまだに中国人民にとっては、毛氏は永遠の神様なのだ。天安門事件で傷を負った鄧小平より、神様をとったのだろう。習氏のしたたかさが見え隠れする。

毛沢東は自らの実体験から学び(self − education)、その思想を共産主義と名付けコミュニズムの中国訳としたようである。毛沢東の凄いところである。だからソ連邦にも評価されたのである。フランス・パリ仕込みの中国名家出身の周恩来や鄧小平などのインテリの共産主義は、毛沢東・四人組には解らなかったのではないかと思う。

ここで、鄧小平について語るべきことがある。彼は姓名から、客家の出身であろう。北方の漢民族で客家語を話し(通常の中国人には、分からない)、縦横の連絡が密でかなり絆が深く強い。客家出身の政治家には、孫文をはじめ、李鵬、台湾の李登輝(台湾)、シンガポールのリー・クワンユー、タイ国のタクシンなど大物が多い。その絆による理よりも情の連携は、我々には知る由もない。鄧小平もその恩恵を受けたに違いない。

dong, and that it was his father who advanced Deng Xiaoping's reform initiatives, thus effectively praising both, Mao Zedong and Deng Xiaoping.

This is where, a call to pause from Deng Xiaoping's son, Deng Pufang. "However, the recent Mr. Xi, after centralizing power and becoming President for Life, there are indications that he is proceeding with strategic economics (price regulations). Shouldn't the market economics (marketisation through allowing national corporations be controlled by the public) that my father initiated be put forward."(Financial Times, November 16th, 2018). In reality, there are incidents in which President Xi has altered the system of the Deng Xiaoping period back to the Mao Zedong period approach. In many respects, Mao Zedong is still seen as an eternal divine entity among the Republic of China's people. Compared to Deng Xiaoping who was scarred by the Tiananmen Square protests, it is better to go with a divine entity. The shrewdness of President Xi can be seen.

Mao Zedong was self-educated by his own experience, and he named his ideals as 'Kyo San Shugi' a Chinese translation for communism. This is where Mao Zedong was exceptional. This is why he was highly evaluated by the Soviet Union. Zhou Enlai, experiencing studies in Paris, France and hailing from a renowned family, and Deng Xiaoping represent the communist elite, I think that it is highly likely that Mao Zedong and the Gang of Four would have difficulty comprehending such individuals.

There is something that I must mention about Deng Xiaoping. Judging from his full name, an assumption can be made that he is member of the 'Hakka', which are of the Han race of the north who speak the 'Hakka' language (conventional Chinese would not understand), have closely knitted relations that run strong and deep. There are numerous influential Hakka people, such as; the politician Sun Yat-sen, Lie Peng, Taiwan's Lie Teng-hui, Singapore's Lee Kuan Yew, and Thai's Taksin Shinawatra. The bond alliance of emotion over reason is beyond our understanding. Deng Xiaoping certainly must have benefited from this bond.

# 第22話

初出：2019年3月25日

# レック・ワレサ（Lech Walesa）と グダニスク（ポーランド北部）

© PA Photos/amanaimages

*Lech Walesa*
レック・ワレサ(1943～)

ポーランドとくれば、ショパン（Frederic Francois Chopin）のピアノとくる。

筆者にとっては1980年代にワルシャワを訪れた時である。国際純正応用化学連合の医薬化学部門の日本代表をしていた頃であるが、ショパンの生地（旧ポーランド貴族）である広大なお屋敷で韓国女性ピアニストのショパンのピアノ曲を聴いたのを鮮明に覚えている。

ところが、ポーランド・グダニスクとくると、最近は物騒な話が多い。市長のパベウ・アダモビッチ（Pawel Adamowicz）が演説中に後ろから刺され（2019年1月13日）、必死の治療のかいもなく翌朝亡くなられた。グダニスクは町全体が喪に服した（in mourning for Pawel）。現在のポーランド政府は超保守派と呼ばれるマイノリティに冷たい政権である。アダモビッチ氏は2018年の市長選挙で政権派の候補者に勝利した野党：シビック・プラットフォーム（Civic Platform）の出身だったのである。分裂は避けたいところである。国家の連帯を祈りたい。

またグダニスクといえば、筆者にとっては往年のレック・ワレサ（Lech Walesa）である。1980年、共産主義全盛の政府に抵抗をして非共産党系の「連帯（Solidarity）」を結成した。当時、筆者は帰国後日本企業（三菱系）に居たが何かしたくてムズムズしていた頃である。彼の不屈の精神力と行動に感動したのだろうか、程なくして筆者も外資系（米国）に転職をした。

Narrative 22

# Lech Walesa and Gdansk (northern Poland)

© 共同通信社/アマナイメージズ

When one thinks of Poland, the piano of Frederic Francois Chopin comes to mind.

For me, I recall when I visited Warsaw in the 1980s. Although it was a period when I was representing the Pharmaceutical Chemical Division of the International Pure Applied Chemistry Union, I vividly recall a Korean pianist and her performance of one of Chopin's pieces which was held at an enormous estate which was Chopin's birthplace.

However, when one thinks of Poland, one envisions Gdansk, where recently unsavory incidents are abundant. On January 13, 2019, Mayor Pawel Adamowicz was stabbed during a speech, despite treatment efforts, he died the following morning. The entire town of Gdansk was in mourning for Pawel. The current Polish government's administration is uncaring toward the minority group that is referred to as the ultra-conservatives. Mr. Adamowicz ran as a representative of the Civic Platform minority party, in the mayoral election last year (2018) and was victorious against the government party candidate. If at all possible, division should be avoided. I pray that the nation will experience solidarity.

In addition, Gdansk reminds me of Lech Walesa of the past. In 1980, he formed Solidarity a freedom-oriented social movement union, in resistance to the over-all Communist government. At the time, after I returned to Japan and was employed by a Japanese firm (Mitsubishi related), and a was experiencing a feeling of unrest. It was highly likely that I was moved by his indomitable spiritual strength and spirit, for before long, I decided to be employed by an American firm.

Lech was arrested in 1981 when martial law was imposed, and Solidarity was out-lawed, resulting in a long time in custody. Perhaps it was due to the fact that he was a non-resistance believer, or the culture of Poland, the Communist government allowed his wife to make peri-

彼は、1981年の戒厳令で拘束され、連帯は非合法化され、長らく留置所暮らしをすることになった。非抵抗主義者だったためか、ポーランドの文化か、共産政権も夫人に対して定期的に拘置所訪問を認めたのである。しかも彼は、カソリックだったので、ほぼ2年ごとに子供を授かり信仰心が篤く家族の絆を大切にした。このような共産主義体制への抵抗活動の最中でも、である。

1983年にはノーベル平和賞を受賞し、ベルリンの壁崩壊（1989年11月9日）後の新世界の幕開けとともに90年には直接選挙で大統領に選ばれた。彼のこのような不屈の活動は他のソ連体制下の諸国にも大きな影響を与えた。ワレサ氏は2000年に政界を引退したが、世界を回り啓蒙に努めている。

ところで、ポーランドが非常な親日国であることをご存知であろうか。今から200年近く前の話である。1831年、帝政ロシアからの独立を計画し武装蜂起をしたころである。多くのポーランド人が政治犯として極寒の雪降るシベリアで強制労働を強いられた。程なくしてロシア革命が起き、レーニン（ウラジミール・レーニン）の主導のもと共産主義ロシア（赤軍）となり、スターリン（ヨシフ・スターリン）によりソビエト連邦が成立した。折りしもこの共産主義ソ連邦成立に干渉すべく当時の国際連盟がシベリアに出兵した。英国や米国などとともに日本も出兵していた。多くのポーランド人が戦死し、多くの孤児（765人）が残された。国際連盟は、地理的に近い日本にその保護を依頼し、日本政府の意向もあり、この孤児たち全員（765人）を無事日本に連れ帰った。日本赤十字が中心となり手厚く保護をしたという。いざ孤児たちが祖国ポーランドに戻るとき、戻りたくないと泣きポーランド国歌と君が代を歌ったという。なんとも辛く、しかし癒される風情である。以来、ポーランドは欧州一の親日国になったと言われている。

これから、良好な米国関係を維持し、共産主義嫌いのポーランドが中国との関係をどのように構築していくのかも見ものである。期待をしたい。

odical visits to the jail in which he was being held. In addition, he was Catholic, almost every two years the couple was blessed with a child, which tells of his strong belief in his faith and the how he treasured the bond of the family. This was all during his resistance activities toward the Communist regime.

In 1983 he was awarded with the Nobel Peace Prize, after the fall of the Berlin wall (November 9th, 1989) it was the beginning of a new world, and in 1990 he was the first President to be elected by popular vote. His indomitable actions had a significant impact on other countries that were under the Soviet Union regime. Although Mr. Walesa has retired from the world of politics in 2000, he travels around the world, striving to enlighten those he meets.

By the way, are you aware that Poland is an extremely pro-Japanese country? The story goes back approximately 200 years ago. In 1831, the Polish planned an armed revolt for independence from imperial Russia. Many Polish, as political prisoners were taken to snow packed, freezing Siberia and put into forced labor. Shortly after the Russian Revolution started, through the leadership of Vladimir Lenin, it became Communist Russia (Red Army), and Josef Stalin established the Soviet Union. It was during this time, as an interference to the establishment of the Communist Soviet Union, the then League of Nations sent troops to Siberia. In addition to British, American, Japanese troops were also sent in. Many Polish perished in this war, and many orphans (765) remained. The League of Nations, due to its geographical proximity, placed a request to Japan to safeguard these orphans, and with the intentions of Japan's government, all 765 orphans were safety taken to Japan. The Japanese Red Cross playing a central role, it is said that the utmost care was provided. When it was time for the orphans to return to their homeland of Poland, while crying that they did not want to return, they sang the Polish national anthem and the Japanese national anthem. What a heartbreaking, however comforting spirit. It is said that, from then on, Poland is the most pro-Japan country in Europe.

From now on, while maintaining its good relationship with the United States, how Poland, which dislikes communism will establish a relationship with China, will be something to watch. I hold expectations.

# 第23話

初出：2019年4月8日

# ウィルムット博士 ——クローン羊ドリーの父

*Sir Ian Wilmut & Dolly the Sheep*
ウィルムット博士とクローン羊ドリー

1997年2月23日、ウィルムット博士(Sir Ian Wilmut)はクローン羊ドリー(Dolly the Sheep)の誕生を報じた。今からほぼ22年前である。衝撃が世界中に飛び、それでは人(ヒト)でもと…。

ウィルムット博士は1944年に英国(Hampton Lucy)に生まれ、ノッティンガム大学(University of Nottingham)を卒業後、ケンブリッジ大学(University of Cambridge)で博士号(Ph.D.)取得。専門は発生学(『Stedman's医学大辞典』によると、卵子の受精から子宮外または卵外生活期までの生物の発生および発育に関する科学)。

当然、数多くの賞(Awards)に恵まれたが、ノーベル賞受賞にはいまだ至っていない。発生学関連のノーベル医学・生理学賞は、山中伸弥教授、ウィルムット博士とガードン博士(Sir John B. Gurdon)と予想されていたが、現実にはウィルムット博士は外れた(2012年)。いつの日か、機会の来るのを祈りたい。

この時のノーベル賞に関して、すさまじい出来事があった。同じ発生学の専門家キャンベル博士(Keith Campbell)は、受賞に外れたことで自らの命を絶った。58歳であった。彼は英国人の母とスコットランド人の父との間に生まれたが、彼の激しい気性は父親のスコティッシュ魂から来ているのかとも思う。ウィルムット博士によると、ドリー誕生には

Narrative 23

# Dr. Wilmut, Father to the Clone Dolly the Cloned Sheep

© Polaris/amanaimages

Roughly 22 years ago, on February 23, 1997, Sir Ian Wilmut disclosed the birth of Dolly the cloned sheep. Shock waves traveled the world over, what about this research going into the realm of humans?

Dr. Wilmut was born in 1944 in Hampton Lucy, Warwickshire, England. After completing studies at the University of Nottingham, he went on to the University of Cambridge to earn a Ph.D. He specialized in embryology (according to Stedman's medical dictionary; it is the branch of biology that studies the prenatal development of gametes (sex cells), fertilization, and development of embryos and fetuses). Naturally, he was the recipient of many awards, the Nobel Prize has yet to be awarded. Although it was predicted that an embryology related Nobel Prize in Physiology or Medicine would go to Professor Shinya Yamanaka and Sir John B. Gurdon, excluding Dr. Wilmut (year 2012). I pray that one day the opportunity will arrive.

In regards to that year's Nobel Prize, a horrifying event occurred. A specialist of the same embryology, Dr. Keith Campbell, unable in receiving the Nobel Prize, took his own life. He was 58 years old. He was born to an English mother and Scottish father, and perhaps it was Scottish spirit inherited from his father that was the source of his intense temperament. According to Dr. Wilmut, he recalled that Dr. Campbell's contribution to the birth of Dolly was immense. Notedly, in 2008 Professor Yamanaka, Dr. Wilmut and Dr. Campbell these three

キャンベル博士の功績が多大であったと述懐している。ちなみに2008年には、山中教授、ウィルムット博士とキャンベル博士が3人でショウ・プライズ（Shaw Prize：香港メディア王と呼ばれたラン・ラン・ショウ（Run Run Shaw）により2002年に創設された賞である。宇宙学、生命科学・医学、数物科学の3分野の賞であり、各受賞に120万米ドルが与えられる）を受賞している。

なぜ、ノーベル賞委員会は、ウィルムット博士とキャンベル博士を外したのだろうか。筆者の推定では、ノーベル賞は受賞者は3人までと決まっており、この2人は甲乙つけ難く外したか、あるいはドリー誕生は科学（science）ではなく技術（engineering）とみなしたかであろう。いずれにしてもノーベル賞候補者に名が挙がると、自らの葛藤は計り知れないものがある。しかし、耐えてこそ・生きてこそ人（ヒト）である。ヒトであることを止めてはいけない。

ノーベル賞を決めるのは、候補者でもなければ、ジャーナリストでもなく、ブックメーカーでもない、ノーベル賞選考委員会である。

そういえば、1962年にワトソン、クリック、ウイルキンス（Watson、Crick、Wilkins）がノーベル医学・生理学賞を受賞した時も、命を失った人がいたのを記憶している。

それでは、日本ではクローニングはどのように応用されているのだろうか。最近（2018年7月）クローニングされた牛（和牛）の卵子を中国に持ち出すという事件があった。中国のある筋は欲しくてたまらないのだ、この卵子を。危険を冒しても、一攫千金を夢見る人間は、いつの世にも存在するのである。人間のさがである。ただ卵子を運ぶ装置は頑丈で重く空港ではすぐ発覚する。そこで船便を利用するわけであるが、今回は中国の税関が気付き、幸い水際で差し止めとなったのである。日本側の男性も刑事事件として立件されている。日中両国の協同作業の良好な結果でもある。

men are awarded the Shaw Prize; established by the Hong Kong media mogul (Run Run Shaw) in 2002. There are three categories of the award; cosmology, life sciences/medical science, and mathematical sciences, each award has a prize of 1.2 million dollars.

Why did the Nobel Committee exclude Dr. Wilmut and Dr. Campbell? I assume that it was either the limitation rule that only three individuals can be awarded, and facing the difficulty of making a decision between the two, may have dictated the Committee's decision, or the Committee may have viewed the birth of Dolly a result of engineering and not science. Whatever the reason, the psychological inner conflict of an individual whose name has been announced as a potential candidate for the Nobel Prize is immeasurable. However, it is withstanding, perseverance and living is what makes us human. Ceasing to be human should not be done.

The decision of who will ultimately receive a Nobel Prize is not a candidate, not a journalist, or bookmakers, it is the Nobel Committee.

Come to think about it, in 1962 when Watson Crick Wilkins was awarded the Nobel Prize for Physiology or Medicine, I recall that there was an individual who lost his life.

Well, let us look at how cloning was applied in Japan. Recently, July of 2018, there was an incident in where the ovum (or egg cell) of a cloned 'Wagyu' cow was taken out of the country to China. There are certain groups of people in China with an immense desire and need to get their hands on these eggs. Ignoring the dangers involved, there are always have been individuals who dream of becoming overnight millionaires. It is human nature. The apparatus necessary to properly transport these eggs would be sturdy and heavy making it immediately discovered at an airport. Thus, shipping it would have been the method of transport, fortunately this time it was discovered by the Chinese customs authorities, which stopped it from entering China. The man responsible in Japan was prosecuted with criminal charges. This successful outcome is the result of the collaboration between the Japanese and Chinese authorities.

## 第24話

初出：2019年5月13日

# おめでとう——カムバックTiger！

© UPI/amanaimages

*Tiger Woods*
タイガー・ウッズ

オミゴト、タイガー！信じられない力強いタイガーの復活。しかもオーガスタ(Augusta)である。タイガー(Tiger Woods)、いつもの赤いシャツに黒ズボンで、例の右腕ガッツ・ポーズも出て最高の一瞬だった。米国が、世界が待っていた瞬間だった。

ちょっと待ってよ。米国大陸には虎(タイガー)は生息していない。なのにタイガー？

タイガーの父、アール・ウッズ(Earl Woods)は1932年に米国カンザス州で生まれ、2006年に74歳で没している。彼はウッズ少年(Eldrick Tont Woods)をプロゴルファーにするため幼少から練習に連れ出し励まし、母親のクルチダ・ウッズ(Kultida Woods)はトーナメントごとに会場までドライブしたという。コース外(オフ・コース、Off Course)での彼女の貢献は大きい。彼女はタイ国生まれで、アール・ウッズが米国軍人としてタイ国に滞在中に結婚したという(1969年)。そして米国カリフォルニア州で生まれたのがウッズ少年である(1975年12月30日)。その名はEldrickを父親からの欧名、そしてTontを母親からタイ名をもらってEldrick Tont Woodsとなった次第である。ウッズ氏は1996年、

## Narrative 24

# Congratulating Tiger for the Comeback!

© Sipa Press/amanaimages

Fantastic, Tiger! An unbelievably strong rally, and of at no less Augusta. Tiger Woods, in his trademark red shirt and black slacks, and shooting up his right hand in a victorious reaction is a wonderful sight. A moment that the United States., and the world was waiting for.

Wait a minute. The tiger does not inhabit the American continent, so why Tiger?

Tiger's father, Earl Woods was born in Kansas State of the U.S. in 1932, and passed away at the age of 74 in 2006. To shape the young Eldrick Tont Woods into a professional golfer, he took and encouraged him to practice, and Tiger's mother, Kultida Woods, would drive him to tournaments. Her contributions were significant off course. She was born in Thailand and married Earl Woods in 1969, while he was in the military stationed in the country. Then on December 30th, 1975, Eldrick Tont Woods was born in the state of California. The western name, Eldrick was given by his father, and Tont is a Thai name given to him by his mother, resulting in the full name of Eldrick Tont Woods. At the age of 21, in 1996 he legally changed

21歳の誕生日にタイガーと法的に名を変更している。しかし出生時の姓名はそのままである。

彼の輝かしいゴルフ歴を語るつもりはない。皆さまの方がはるかに詳しいはずである。彼の人間というか、苦労と苦難の中でどのようにしてこの復活を成し遂げたのかを見てみたい。彼一人で復活を果たしたのではない、多くの人のサポートがあっての賜物であるから。

彼は2004年10月にエリン・ノルデグレン(Elin Nordegren)と最初の結婚をしている。彼女はスウェーデン系女性としてフロリダでモデルの仕事をしていた。彼は結婚にあたり、サンディ・レーン・リゾート(Sandy Lane Resort)を1週間借り切り200万ドル(約2億円)をかけたという。彼女についてはメディアの中傷もあったが、2007年長女 サム・アレクシス・ウッズ(Sam Alexis Woods)が誕生している。2009年は、長男チャーリー・アクセル・ウッズ(Charlie Axel Woods)が誕生している。しかし、彼がフロリダの自宅近くの道路で自損事故を起こし、家庭生活に専念するために、ゴルフから離れるとまで公表したが、さらにスキャンダルも公になり、彼女がタイガーを許さず。2010年8月23日に正式に離婚届けを提出した。彼女の腕利きの弁護士である姉妹ジョセフィン(Josefin)の手助けもあり、慰謝料は1億ドル(約100億円)。ハイ、一丁上がり！

もちろん、タイガーが今回復活を果たしたのは、現在のベターハーフ(恋人)であるエリカ・ハーマン(Erica Herman)のお陰である。持つべき者は、ともに良き理解者ということ。

ここでタイガーの心(こころ)の優しさに触れたい。自死を企てているという少年を知るに及んで、彼は手紙を書いた。僕も少年の時吃音があり、犬に話しかけるとその犬は彼が眠るまでジッと聞いていてくれたと。忍耐を説かれた少年もまた救われたという。タイガーもまた人(ヒト)として達人である。

最後に触れたいのは、彼のサイン入りの大きなカラー写真が筆者の居間の壁に掛かっている。

his Thai name to Tiger, retaining his first name and last name from birth, thus he is known as Eldrick Tiger Woods.

I have no intention of writing about his outstanding achievements as a golf professional, for I firmly believe that many of you are far more informed on than me. I would like to look into, as a human being, he succeeded in overcoming numerous ordeals and achieve a comeback. He certainly did not achieve this comeback alone; it is the result of the many people who supported him.

His first marriage was to Elin Nordegren in October of 2004. She is of Norwegian descent and was working as a model in Florida. In preparing for the wedding, Tiger spent an estimated 2 million dollars (an estimated 200 million yen) to book the Sandy Lane Resort for one week. Although there was a certain amount of unfavorable media coverage of Elin, in 2007 there was the birth of their daughter Sam Alexis Woods. In 2009, their son Charlie Axel Woods was born. However, Tiger upon causing a car accident involving damages near his home in Florida, announced that he was going to take time away from golf to focus more upon his family. A further scandal came into light, which Elin could not forgive Tiger, leading to her filing for a divorce on August 23, 2010. Receiving the professional counsel of her sister Josefin, who is a skilled attorney, Elin was awarded an alimony amounting to 100 million dollars (an estimated 10 billion yen). Well, one up!

Of course, the comeback this time made by Tiger was with the help of his current better half, Erica Herman. An exceptional individual is endowed with an individual who possesses great understanding.

At this point I would like to touch upon the kindness of Tiger's heart. When learning of a young man who had tried to take his own life, Tiger wrote a letter. In it he wrote, 'When I was young, I had a stammer, when I would talk to my dog, the dog would dutifully listen until I went to sleep.' Upon receiving this example in perseverance, the young man is said to have been saved. Tiger is also a master as a human being.

Lastly, I will divulge that on my living room wall there is a large signed color photograph of Tiger.

## 第25話

# 世界が回る――バイオ通訳のトップランナー 北山ユリ女史と椎野幸子女史

世界を飛び回るSuper-Class通訳の北山ユリ女史（北山さん）と椎野幸子女史(椎野さん)には、大変お世話になってきた。

まず、通訳の仕事が、「いかに過酷なものか」を説明したい。

1. 通訳を頼まれると、内容の資料をすべて紙媒体で要求し、前もって勉強をしておく。だから、Super-Classの北山さん・椎野さんが、通常のサイエンティスト（科学者）の知識並み or それ以上のものを有しているのも頷ける。
2. さらに、一人の通役がカヴァーできるのは、30分までである。30分以上は、二人の通訳が必須である。しかも、そのコンビネーションが、うまく回らないといけない。
3. だから、二人の組み合わせを「どのようにして頼むか」は、頼む側の「通訳の方々の性格・人脈の広さをどのくらい知っているか」が問われることになる。事実として、小生は北山さんと椎野さんのコンビを頼んだことがない。タイプは違うが、お互いの強いリーダーシップがかみ合わない時もあるかもしれないから……。

北山さんは、中学時代から浅利慶太氏の通訳をしていたという。北山さんも椎野さんも、その正義感・倫理観と強いリーダーシップで 緊急の依頼でも（2～3日）、通訳の手配を全国に声を掛け、優秀で一流の翻訳者を用意していただける。自らもたびたび通訳の任を受け持ってくれる。アサシス社のCEO、ギル・ヴァン・ボッケレン（Gil Van Bokkelen）や、北大総長の寶金先生も非常に高く評価されている。「彼女たちなら」とい

## Narrative 25

# Top–runners of bio-translation: Miss Yuri Kitayama and Miss Sachiko Shiino have been jumping around Australia–The UK–The US–Asia

*Yuri Kitayama*
北山ユリ

*Sachiko Shiino*
椎野幸子

Looking around 360 degrees in the world, Mrs. Yuri Kitayama and Mrs.Sachiko Shiino have been famous in the world, as the top-runner in bio-translates.

Would like to explain the toughness of translation even from to English or vis viva.

First, 1. when translates are requested to be the opportunity to be translates, they request clients to provide all documents in all in paper. They have started immediately to study them, and themselves to try to finds relevant documents. The both of Kitayama san and Shiino san have knowledges similar or more to regular scientists. It' s reasonable.

2. Secondary, one translate is able to cover only 30 minutes, and over the 30 minutes, Therefor absolutely needed two or more translates.

3. The clients also would be tested and required as well that how widely know relationship and communications among translates. So that I have not yet to arrange Kitayama san and Shiino san, while they are a good friend each othre. Please understand it. Some may not be understanding the situation. Can' t help.

つも喜んでくれる。さらにお二人とも、元米国メルク社で現在アサシス社の国際的規制のプロであるマナル・モルシ女史（Dr. Manal Morsy）とは、厚労省・PMDAにおける会議の数々を通じて長いお付き合いが続いている。とにかく掛けた情けが長続きするのである、お二人は。

北山さんは、東京生まれで中・高・大は青山学院。子供時代の北山さんは、破天荒だ。北山さんは幼少時、負けず嫌いで鳴らしたみたいである。兄上は、佛教大学を出たが、医学部に入りなおし、病院勤務の医者でもある。

椎野さんも東京まれの東京育ち。都立高から語学で有名な私大を卒業している。背が高く品格のある方である。話しぶりも穏やかだ。お二人とも、世界を飛び回り、こなした国内外の会議は、数えきれない。

最後になるが、椎野さんと絶妙なコンビを組んでいた小林しのぶさんや日渡さんにも、触れたい。しのぶさんは、オランダ語の通訳もできる。皆、素晴らしい人たちである。すべてに感謝である。益々の発展・ご自愛を祈ってやまない。

Mrs. Kitayama in Junior-High was the translate of Mr. Keita Asari, a very famous stage director. Kitayama san and Shiino san, based on strong Justice and ethics and a strong leadership, I asked translates even in a couple of days in advance, arranged a first-class translates on time.

Kitayama san and Shiino san have been trusted so deeply by Dr. Gill Van Bokkelen, CEO Athersys Company in Ohio and The Chancellor of Hokkaido University, Dr. Kiyotaka Houkin. They have been always most welcomed as translates.

Especially, Dr. Manal Morsy once in Merck now in Athersys, a world-famous regulatory professional has trusted them through the translations at MHLW and PMDA as well.

Their trusty has been continued as long among the business partners. Kitayama san born in Tokyo graduated from famous Ayoyama-Gakuin from Junior high through University.

But, Kitayama san was crazy in child,disliking being defeated. And his brother was once in Buddhism, then became a physician now in a hospital.

Shiino also born in Tokyo, through a Tokyo-City High School,graduated a famous University in English Course. She is tall and sounds elegant. And she is talking softly and nicely.

Would like to refer to Miss Shinobu Kobayashi that have been making the amicable combination in translations with Shiino san, and to Miss Hiwatari. Shinobu san ables to be a translate for Dutch.

They are going to be more developed, and a good luck, hope and believe I.

## 第26話

初出：2019年7月8日

# 本田 圭佑——戦争をなくしたい

© ZUMA Press/amanaimages

*Keisuke Honda*
本田圭佑（1986 ～）

驚きの一言「戦争をなくしたい」。最近のTV番組でこれから何をしたいかと問われ、彼が言った言葉である。

氏が個人としてまたチームとして世界を巡る時、巡り合う人々や子供たちは紛争や戦争と隣り合わせの困難な環境で我慢の生活をしている。その本質を解決できないモドカシさ、個人ではどうにもならないモドカシさから出た本音であろう。実体験のない筆者には新鮮な感動の言葉である。

氏のサッカーについて語る資格はないが、その雄姿は鮮烈である。ロングシュートやクルクル回るドリブルは見ていて楽しい。おそらく、F1ドライバーの中嶋悟氏が信号で停車してクルリと周りを見ると、鳥瞰図的に自分の車の位置が浮かぶという話と同じで、本田氏も瞬間瞬間で鳥瞰図的に自分の位置を把握しているのだろう。もちろん、カズ氏（三浦知良）や中田英寿氏もそうであろうし、長谷部誠氏もそうだ。要するに眼球、頭そして敵味方の区別のついた周りのプレーヤー(s)との駆け引きと連携にウルトラ・スーパーなのである。

中田英寿氏と本田圭佑氏は違う。中田氏の世界的な活動・躍動そしてフィランソロピックな（博愛）優しさと違って、本田氏のそれはもっと

## Narrative 26

# Keisuke Honda —— Ridding the World of War

© ZUMA Press/amanaimages

A surprising statement [Ridding the World of War]. In a recent television program, when asked what he wanted to do henceforward, he voiced this statement.

Through his travels around the globe individually or with his team, gave him a look at children who live near or next to areas of conflict, making an extremely difficult environment in which the children are forced to endure. Frustrated from not being able to find a solution to the essence of the problem, as well as the frustration that comes from perceiving the limitation, as one individual, his honest emotions were voiced in this statement. For one who has not actually experienced this, the statement made a fresh emotion.

Although he may not possess the qualifications to speak about soccer, his splendid figure on the pitch is vivid. It was a great pleasure watching him make long shoots or do dribbles while circling. It may be similar to how the F1 driver Satoru Nakajima has stated, that while awaiting for the green light, he can mentally visualize with a bird's eye view the area surrounding the position of his car, Mr. Honda can spontaneously, with a bird's eye view, perceive his position. Of course, Kazu (Kazuyoshi Miura) and Hidetoshi Nakata have the same capability,

直接的であるような気がする。フーという息が聞こえそうな感じ。

本田氏は、モスクワのCSKAをはじめACミランではエース・ナンバー10を付け、時々ユニホームの肩を持ち上げアピールする姿が印象的であった。氏は現在、筆者の第二の故郷であるオーストラリアのメルボルン・ビクトリーで活躍している。語学も堪能という。またカンボジアのナショナル・チームの監督もしていると聞いた。そのエネルギーは、どこから来るのか。両親に感謝と家族に感謝なのか。自らの鍛錬も並ではなさそうである。

本田氏は1986年大阪の摂津市で生まれている。2008年オランダの一部リーグ(Eredivisie)VVVフェンロー(VVV − Venlo)に2年半の契約で入団。時に22歳である。驚くことに若い時から将来のサッカー選手を目指して英会話の勉強に励み英語に堪能な吉田麻也氏を誘い、吉田氏は入団した。まさに実力者が実力者を同じチームに誘いストラグルする醍醐味を経験するのである。清々しいスポーツマンシップの世界である。ジェラシーなど入る余地もない。本当の実力がないとできないことである。時を経て吉田氏はオール・ジャパンの主将を任せられるまでになった。

本田氏やマンU(Manchester United)でハットトリックをした香川真司氏、そして新キャプテンの吉田氏、岡崎慎司氏、イタリアで活躍中の長友佑都氏も30歳チョットとまだ若い。東京オリンピックではここぞという場面での期待を込めてオーバーエイジ枠でベンチ入りすることであろう。

ジャパン・ナショナル・チームの監督である森保一氏に率いられる若手のサッカー選手の優秀さは、海外組・国内組ともすごい選手がおり海外遠征などでも証明済みである。オリンピックやワールドカップでは経験豊かな先輩組とともに活躍してほしい。監督も試合ごとにプレーヤーの選択に苦労するであろう。成功を祈るとともに、見るのが楽しみである！

as well as Makoto Hasebe. What this reflects is the superhuman capability of these individuals' eyes, brain to differentiate team members and opponent players, coordinate and execute tacticsto win the game.

Hidetoshi Nakata and Keisuke Honda are different. In contrast to Mr. Nakata's global scale activities and energetic philanthropic kindness, I feel that Mr. Honda's activities are more direct. It is as though you can hear a breath being exhaled.

Mr. Honda, starting with Moscow's CSKA, went on the AC Milan wearing the ace number 10, at times pulling at the shoulders of his uniform as an act to appeal was an impressive figure. Current he is active in, what for me is a second hometown, Melbourne Victory of Australia. He is also fluent in languages. I have also heard that he is supervising Cambodia's national team. Where does this energy come from? Perhaps, thankful to his parents and grateful toward his family. His training is known to be exceptional.

Mr. Honda was born in Setsu City of Osaka in 1986. In 2008 he signed a 2 and half contract with part of Holland's league, Eredivisie, VVV-Venlo. He was 22 at the time. What is surprising, at an early age, setting his future goal to become a soccer player, focusing on studying English and becoming fluent, was Maya Yoshida whom he invited, resulting in Mr. Yoshida also joining the club. An accomplished player inviting another accomplished player to struggle within the same team provides the best of experiences. A world of refreshing sportsmanship. No room for jealously to enter the picture. It is only those who have true and real capability to do. As time passed, Mr. Yoshida eventually became captain for the All Japan team.

Mr. Honda, as well as, Shinji Kagawa playing for Manchester United succeeded in a hattrick, the new captain, Mr. Yoshida, Shinji Okazaki, and Yu Nagatomo, who plays in Italy, are slightly over 30, still young. At the Tokyo Olympic Games, they will probably be on the benches as members of the over age group, anticipating a crucial moment.

Japan's National Team, managed by Kazu Moriyasu, is a formed by young soccer players, whose capabilities have been evident with players who represent international and domestic groups, and their skill has been proven through their performance in international arenas. We look forward to their future performance with their forerunner players who have ample experienced from playing within the Olympics and the World Cup. Surely, the manager faces the difficulty of choosing players for respective matches. I pray for their success, as well as look forward to watching!

第27話　初出：2019年7月22日

# スコット・ゴットリーブ(前FDA長官)——ファイザー(米国本社)の社外取締役に就任、何をするの?

© Sipa USA/amanaimages

*Scott Gottlieb*
スコット・ゴットリーブ

ゴットリーブ氏(MD、Ph.D)との出会いは、氏とFDA長官だったレスター・クロフォード氏(D.V.Docter Lester Crawford)、米国研究製薬工業協会(Pharmaceutical Research and Manufacturers of America／PhRMA)の事業担当上級副社長シャノン・グラハム(Shannon Graham)とワシントンDCのオフィスで打ち合わせをした時だった(2005年)。もう14年になる。筆者は、当時PhRMAの対日科学・技術代表であった。日米欧の人脈が急に広がった頃である。ゴットリーブ氏は、テキサス出身でブッシュ家と繋がりのある共和党のヘルスケア界のエースだった人である。物静かで威張った風のない人柄と不退転の意志の強い感じがしたのを覚えている。時を待たず、クロフォード氏が、持ち株(関連企業)によるFDAとの利益相反(Conflict of Interest)で退任を余儀なくされ、FDAを去った。在任は2005年の7月18日から9月23日、わずか2カ月余りであった。惜しい人であった。少しの間長官不在のあと、ゴットリーブ氏が就任したが、すぐに米国疾病予防管理センター(CDC、現在CDCP)に転出。父ブッシュ政権の医療・教育省の長官かと思ったら、父ブッシュがビル・クリントン氏に敗れ、民主党政権となり

Narrative 27

# Scott Gottlieb (former FDA Commissioner) —— Appointed the Pfizer's Board of Directors, what is he going to do?

My encounter with Scott Gottlieb, MD, Ph.D., was in 2005 at a meeting in Shannon Graham, Senior Vice President of Business, Pharmaceutical Research and Manufacturers of America (PhRMA) Washington D.C. office, along with then FDA Commissioner, Lester Crawford, DVM, Ph.D. It was 14 years ago. At the time I was the Science/Technical Representative of PhRMA, Japan. It was a time when I my relationships with Japanese, American and European people rapidly expanded. Mr. Gottlieb, a native of Texas, with relationships with the Bush family, was the Republican Party's healthcare ace. Although possessing a quite disposition, he emitted an air of arrogance, and I specifically recall his unmistakable sense of determination. It was not long after this meeting that Mr. Crawford, as a holder of stocks in related firms, and was found by the FDA to be in a position of conflict of interest, had to resign and leave the FDA. He was commissioner of the FDA from July 18th to September 23rd of 2005, holding the position for slightly more than 2 months. It was regrettable loss. A brief absence occurred, and although Mr. Gottlieb was appointed to the post, he was immediately transferred to the Center for Disease Control and Prevention (CDCP). It was predicted that he would serve as Secretary of Health and Human Services under George H. W. Bush's Administration, however George H.W. Bush lost the presidential election to Bill Clinton, a Democratic administration was established, thus this potential was not realized.

It was this January that after serving as Commissioner, he suddenly announced that he was resigning. This caused a stir to the surroundings. Including Japan! There was a Biotechnology Industry Organization (BIO) mission scheduled to visit Japan in March. I had accompanied the mission to the Prime Minister's official residence, as well as the PMDA, the mission's leader, learning of PMDA Director, Tatsuya Kondo's retirement, thought of recommending his as Mr. Gottlieb's successor. Although this took us by complete surprise, however Director Kondo was happy with what he thought as quite an honor. When the mission visited the PMDA and learned of the Director's fundamental philosophy toward healthcare, and the PMDA's doctrine, they were extremely impressed.

Now, why did Mr. Gottlieb become a member of the Pfizer's Board of Directors? In

実現せず。

またこの1月には2年務めたFDA長官の引退を突然表明。周辺を揺さぶった。日本も含めて！ ちょうど3月に米国BIOのミッションが来日。筆者が官邸、PMDA（医薬品医療機器総合機構）他の案内をしたので、ミッションのトップから同じく退任するPMDA近藤達也理事長（当時）をゴットリーブ氏の後任に推薦したいともちかけられた。こっちもびっくりしたが、近藤理事長も名誉なことだと喜んでくれた。ミッションがPMDAを訪ねた時、理事長のヘルスケアへの基本方針・PMDAの理念に感動したのである。

さてゴットリーブ氏はなぜファイザー社の社外取締役になったのか。今年1月米国ファイザーで10年務めたCEOを退任したイアン・リード氏（Executive Chairman、スコットランド生まれ）、彼と入れ替わりでCEOとなったアルバート・ブーラ氏（Albert Bourla、ギリシャ生まれ）、この6月28日に社外取締役となったゴットリーブ氏の年齢を見ると、何と面白いことに66－56－47ではないか。10年刻みでゴットリーブ氏は年内にCOOそして10年後、CEOになるのは間違いがない。しかも今月（7月）から、ファイザーもトロイカ方式のオペレーションになる。前2者が外国生まれなのに、彼ゴットリーブ氏は米国生まれである。

つまりファイザーは米国にとどまって米国経済に貢献するということである。製薬業界は、もともと共和党支持であるが、トランプ氏の再選にギアを踏み込んだのではないかと思う。

そのファイザーのトロイカ自転車はどこを目指してこぐのか。もちろん、基礎研究に多大の投資をして自ら創薬・開発をしてマーケット部門を後押しし、売上げのトップ維持と利益の上昇を目指す。ウーン、どこかで見た風情だねえー。そうだ！ MSDの“今でしょ”（出所、林修氏）。PD－1（キイトルーダ）そして有効なM＆A（2009年Schering Plough買収、当時の4兆円余）。まあー、このようなシナリオを新ファイザーも考えていると思う。そうでないと、今回のゴットリーブ氏の移動の意味がない。

January of the year, Ian Read, born in Scotland, retired after serving for 10 years as CEO, Executive Chairman, he was succeeded by Albert Bourla, (born in Greece), on June 28th Mr. Gottlieb became a member of the Board of Directors, looking at his age, I discovered something very intriguing, it was the sequence 66-56-47. Divided by 10 years, within the year Mr. Gottlieb will become COO, 10 years later, there is little doubt that he would become CEO. In addition, from this month (July), will adapt the Troika System for operations. The two predecessors were born abroad, Mr. Gottlieb was born in the United States.

This reflects that Pfizer will remain in the United States and contribute to the economy of the U.S. The pharmaceutical industry are traditionally supporters of the Republican Party, I believe that they may be gearing up to get Mr. Trump re-elected.

In what direction will the Pfizer Troika bicycle go? Of course, allocating the largest investment toward basic research and conduct their own drug discovery/development, support and back-up the market division, and aim to sustain top in sales and the increase in profit. Vienna, it reflects a character that I have seen somewhere before. Yes, of course it was MSD's "It is now isn't it" (from Mr. Osamu Hayashi). PD-1(keytruda)and the effective M&A (purchasing Schering Plough at an estimated 4 trillion yen in 2009). Well, I think the new Pfizer is most likely thinking of a similar scenario as well. If not, the recent transition by Mr. Gottlieb will have no meaning.

## 第28話

初出：2020年1月13日

# 黒川　清──日本学術会議第19・20期会長

独特の鼻にかかった高音で話すのが、語りをわかりやすくする（英語・日本語ともに）。内閣特別顧問にも就かれていた黒川先生との出会いは、ハプニングから始まった。米国E.リリー社の日本におけるR＆D責任者であった私は、東海大学医学部長として飛ぶ鳥を落とすほど高名だった先生──東海大学医学部付属病院を2年で黒字化──にE.リリー社のパイプラインを説明しアドバイスを受けたく、ホテルオークラ東京のロビーで夕方6時半に会う約束をした（多分、2005年ごろ）。その時、ロビーを疾風のごとく駆け抜け、例のオークラ特有の奥のスペースに座った方がいた。7時になっても現れないので、ボーイに探してもらおうとしたら、黒川先生はもうあちらにおいでですという。先ほどの紳士ではないか。

自己紹介をして、腎臓内科の大家で東大から米国UCLAで助教、準教授、教授と虹の橋を駆け上がり、東大教授（第一内科）として戻っても、なお夢を追いかけ東海大学医学部長として活躍中の先生とは、予想をは

## Narrative 28

# Kiyoshi Kurokawa —— The Science Council of Japan's 19th & 20th Term Chairman

Speaking in a particularly nasal and high-pitched tone, allows one to understand what is being said (in both English and Japanese). My first encounter with Dr. Kurokawa, who has also held the position of Special Advisor to the Cabinet, started with a happening. At the time I was responsible for R&D in Japan for the U.S. firm Eli Lilly, and was to have a meeting with the extremely well known Dean of the School of Medicine of Tokai University, Dr. Kurokawa – who in 2 years had made the Tokyo University Hospital profitable – to explain Lilly's pipeline as well as receive advice. The appointment was to meet him in the Hotel Okura Tokyo's lobby at 6:30PM (I believe this was in 2005). It was then that a gentleman came rushing into the lobby like a gale, and taking a seat deep within an area especially known to the Okura. Becoming 7PM, with no sight of him, I asked a bell boy to go in search, and was told that Dr. Kurokawa is seated over there. There is no other gentleman as Dr. Kurokawa.

He provided a self-introduction, as an authority on nephrology, he went from the University of Tokyo to becoming an Assistant Professor at the U.S.'s UCLA, going on to becoming Associate Professor, continuing his run across the rainbow bridge, returning as Professor to the University to Tokyo (first department of internal medicine), pursuing his dream while active as the Dean of the School of Medicine Tokai University, he continued to speak of his values in a speed that far exceeded expectations. An extremely spirited individual, who shares his impressions in a straightforward manner. All the while smiling, it was easy to immediately develop a kinship. It felt as though we were speaking in the U.S. Of course, I had spoken to the finance department and had come prepared with an insignificant sum with its tax deducted. He declined saying "This is the first time we met, it's not necessary." He also mentioned that it was good to meet someone who understands the value of time. Regarding Eli Lilly, he highly appraised the firm's decision to wash its hands from antibiotics and had turned its focus toward neuropsychiatry. From this day on, whenever we meet, he raises his hand in greeting. A frank and cordial gentleman.

Many events had taken place in the following years, Dr. Kurokawa was requested by the government to initiate a project with the objective to conceive the direction in which Japan's

るかに超えるスピードと価値観で話が進んだ。とにかく明るくて、ストレートに感想を言ってくれるのである。しかもニコニコしながらなので、一気に親近感が湧く。米国で話している感じになる。もちろん、経理と話して源泉徴収付きの少しばかりの用意をして来ていたが。いいよ、いいよ、そんなの初めて会うんだからという。時間の価値を解かっている人に会えてうれしいとも言ってくれた。E.リリー社についても、抗生物質から足を洗い精神神経方面に舵を切ったのを高く評価してくださった。以来、会うと気軽に手を挙げてくれる。気さくないい方である。

その後いろいろなことがあり、黒川先生は政府から請われて日本の医療をどのような方向に持ってゆくのかを検討するプロジェクトを発足された。私は米国研究製薬工業協会（ワシントンD.C.）の対日技術代表になっていた。君も入れと言われ、藤原先生（現PMDA理事長）なども呼び出された。当時は縛りもなく、藤原先生とは、NIH、FDA、民間の研究所など米国行脚をしたりした。もちろん、報告書は書いた。

さて最近非常に印象に残ったのは、忘れもしない2011年3月12日、私も3時間かけてタワーホール船堀から歩いて東大まで帰ってきた。道すがら店のTVに映る川と化した道路を流れる船や建物を見て、何が起きているのか見当がつかなかった。怒れる自然には、人間は勝てないと悟った。この時、翌3月13日には、国会事故調査委員会が立ち上がり、黒川先生が委員長になった。請求権と国政調査権を与えられ、請求権を使って東電の資料を全部見るという大事業になったが、先生のリーダーシップとスタッフの不屈の魂が報告書（和文・英文）となり、米科学振興協会（AAAS）から「科学の自由と責任賞」（2012年）に選ばれた。そして2012年7月6日、外国記者クラブ（新橋）で提言が生かされていないと、例の嘆きの記者会見となったのである。

また先生は、日本の将来に向けた科学技術政策の確立を目指して設立された政策研究大学大学院の教授となり、提言をまとめ、2009年にアカデミックフェロー、現在は名誉教授である。日本国のために、益々のご活躍を祈って止まない。

healthcare should take. I had become the Technical Representative for Japan of Pharmaceutical Research and Manufacturers of America (Washington D.C.). Dr. Fujiwara (current PMDA chairman), was called upon to join the project. At the time, possessing no restrictions, Dr. Fujiwara had made pilgrimages to the NIH, FDA, and private research institutions in the United States. Of course, he has written reports.

Recently there is an event that has left a strong impression on me, I will never forget the 3 hour walk from Tower Hall Funabori going back to the University of Tokyo on March 12 (11), 2011. Seeing the images projected from storefront television sets of roads transformed into rivers, boats and structures being swept away, I could not absorb what it was that was occurring. I realized the fragility of man against the ferocity of nature. At this time, on March 13th, the Diet established an accident investigation commission, and Dr. Kurokawa became the chairman of this commission. The commission was provided with the right to conduct investigations into governmental affairs, and thus empowered, it received and reviewed all documentation from the Tokyo Electric Power Co., Inc., although a momentous endeavor, but with Dr. Kurokawa's leadership and the staff's indomitable spirit, resulted in a comprehensive report (English and Japanese) which was ultimately received the Award for Scientific Freedom and Responsibility (2012) from the American Association for the Advancement of Science (AAAS). Then on July 6th, 2012, at a press conference held at the Foreign Correspondents Club of Japan (Marunouchi), Dr. Kurokawa lamented on how the recommendations made within the report were not acted upon.

Dr. Kurokawa, with the objective to establishing science technology policies for the future of Japan, founded the National Graduate Institute for Policy Sciences (GRIPS), at which he was professor, after compiling the recommendations, in 2009 he became an Academic Fellow, currently he holds the post of professor emeritus. I pray for his continued contributions for the nation of Japan.

# 第29話

初出：2020年1月27日

# 近藤 達也
## ——米国FDA長官にノミネートされた男

*Dr. T. Kondo PMDA Chief Executive*
近藤達也独立行政法人医薬品医療機器総合機構（PMDA）理事長

2019年3月4日から7日にかけて、米BIO（Biotechnology Innovation Organization）のメンバー約300人が来日した。日本からの参加者約100人として約400人が討論をした。公用語は英語。時のPMDA（医薬品医療機器総合機構）理事長であった近藤達也氏（脳神経外科医）は3月5日にKeynote Speechをして、3月8日にPMDAにて表敬訪問を受けたが、3月31日で退任する話をした。直後にBIOのマネジメントで議論した上で、米国BIOの国際部長モニカ・ヒー（Monica He）から小生に以下のメールが飛び込んできた。

Dear Toshi（Toshi Kobayashi, The University of Tokyo）
Also please ask Dr Kondo if he would be interested
in becoming the Commissioner of the United States
FDA, now that Dr Scott Gottlieb is leaving. We would
definitely like to nominate him for the job！
Monica（Monica He, Director of International of BIO）

とにかく、近藤理事長にその旨伝えねば…。電話で連絡したら、不可能なことだが大変名誉なことだと喜んでくれた。PMDAとしても名誉なことであった。現実は、FDAコミッショナーは、米国の医薬品・ワクチン政策の決定機関であり、NIHと同じく米国人であることが必要条件である。勿論、十分条件ではない。この件でも、近藤前理事長との距離が一気に縮まった。

Narrative 29

# Tatsuya Kondo —— A Man Nominated to Become the Commissioner of the FDA

From March 4th to the 7th, 2019, an estimated 300 members of the American delegates of the Biotechnology Innovation Organization (BIO) came to Japan. Along with roughly 100 participants from Japan, a total of an estimated 400 people held discussions. The official language was English. On this occasion, Mr. Kondo (neurosurgeon), the Chief Executive of the Pharmaceuticals and Medical Devices Agency (PMDA), made the keynote speech on March 5th, and on March 8th he received a courtesy visit by members at the PMDA, at which he disclosed that he would retire on the 31st of March. After immediately holding discussions with BIO management, the email below arrived to me from the U.S. BIO's International Director, Monica.

Dear Toshi (Toshi Kobayashi, The University of Tokyo)
Also please ask Dr Kondo if he would be interested in becoming the Commissioner of the United States FDA, now that Dr Scott Gottlieb is leaving. We would definitely like to nominate him for the job!
Monica (Monica He, Director of International of BIO)

In any case, it was this must be conveyed to Chief Executive Kondo... I made the phone call, in our conversation he said that although the offer is impossible to accept, he felt that it was an extreme honor to be considered of which he was delighted. It is also an honor for the PMDA as well. In reality, the FDA Commissioner is responsible for the organization that decided drug and vaccine policies of the United States, and as with the National Institute of Health (NIH), it is mandatory rule that the post is to be held by an American. Of course, this is not a sufficient condition. In this respect, the distance to Chief Executive Kondo immediately shortened.

From the time I introduced Gil Van Bokkelen, CEO & Chairman of Athersys Inc., to which I am a Senior Strategic Advisor, to Chief Executive Kondo regarding the firm's stem cells

近藤前理事長と、アサシス社(Athersys Inc.)のCEO兼Chairmanのギル・ヴァン・ボッケレン氏(Gil Van Bokkelen)は、ギルの専任上級戦略アドヴァイザーである小生がアサシス社の幹細胞であるステムセル(Stem Cell)の脳梗塞への臨床開発(先駆け・オーファン・ドラッグ取得済/公知)に向けて引き合わせて以来、ある意味で親友となった。時に近藤理事長は、再生医療の日本における発展に、大変興味を持っていたからである。ギルも再生医療を話し出したら、エンドレス。PMDAを訪ねるたびに議論が弾んだ。臨床開発に向け、PMDAでアサシス社幹部、ライセンス先の企業(H社)と事前面談、対面助言を繰り返し、ヤッと臨床開発に滑り込むまで約2年。今年(2020年)1月1日、患者エンロールが105例に到達した。

近藤氏が10余年にわたって務めたPMDA理事長を退任された後、FDA長官の件もあり「3T会+1」という名の親睦会を創(つく)ろうかということになった。近藤達也のTatsuya、布施敏夫(善美写真館オーナー)のToshio、小生のToshi、そしてバイオ翻訳界のトップスター、北山ユリさんである。よって、「3T会+1」である。布施氏の従兄が近藤前理事長の同級生(脳外)で大の親友であった。が、今は故人。

この「3T会+1」が開かれる場所が、隠れ家「寿司正」である。寿司正数あれど、我(われら)が寿司正は、西新橋である。下戸のマエストロで礼儀を心得た正兄(まさあに)が仕切り、奥さんが手伝うオシドリ夫婦である。座敷もよし、カウンターもよしである。奥さんは、煮物も得意でベジタリアンOKである。

近藤前理事長の魅力は、脳神経外科の専門家として50年余の他に、ドイツのMax Planck Instituteにおいて基礎研究をしたということや、国立国際医療(研究)センターの病院長を5年も務めたという事実である。医薬品、医療機器も扱うPMDAにふさわしい人物・人材だったのである。

for cerebral infarction clinical development, (Pioneer Status/Orphan Drug obtained/officially known), in a sense we have become good friends. At the time, Chief Executive Kondo was extremely interested in the development of regenerative medicine in Japan. Gil, when he starts talking about regenerative medicine, it becomes endless. Whenever a visit is made to the PMDA, active discussions became the norm. In progressing toward clinical development, at the PMDA, executives of Athersys, representatives of the licensee corporation (H- Corporation) had repeatedly met for preliminary meetings, as well as, face-to-face counseling, resulting in finally receiving the approval to conduct clinical development after an estimated 2 years. As of January 1st, of this year (2020), they have achieved a patient enrollment of 105 cases.

Mr. Kondo, after retiring from the position of chief executive of the PMDA, which he has held for 10 odd years, regarding the possibility of becoming the commissioner of the FDA, an idea arose to found a convivial group named [3T + 1] Club. Tatsuya Kondo's Tatsuya, Toshio Fuse (the owner of the Yoshimi Photo Studio) Toshio, and my own name Toshi, and the top star of the bio translators, Yuri Kitayama. Resulting in [3T + 1] Club. Mr. Fuse's cousin (neurosurgeon) was a classmate, as well as, great friend of Chief Executive Kondo. However, unfortunately deceased.

The venue for the meeting of [3T + 1] Club is a hideout; the [Sushi Masa]. There may be numerous Sushi Masa's, our Sushi Masa is located in Nishi Shimbashi. The non-drinking maestro, manages with ease with ingrained courtesy, with his wife assisting, they are an ideal couple. The sitting room is good, as is the counter seats. His wife is excellent at Japanese style stewed vegetables, making it ideal for vegetarians as well.

What makes former Chief Executive Kondo exceptional is; added to his 50 odd years as a specialist in the field of neurosurgery, is his basic research at Germany's Max Planck Institute, and his 5-year tenure as the president of the National Center for Global Health and Medicine. He was indeed the ideal individual to oversee the PMDA, which dealt with pharmaceuticals and medical devices.

左から
元厚労省審議官：
俵木登美子氏
山本 文氏
中垣正幸氏

## 第30話

初出：2020年3月9日

# PMDA理事長 藤原 康弘
# ——藤原先生、SOSです

第29話でも少し触れたが、筆者が米国研究製薬工業協会(PhRMA、ワシントンD.C)の対日技術代表をしていたころ、PMDAの現理事長である藤原氏はPMDAにおける日本医学会(高久史麿会長)代表として佐瀬一洋現順天堂大学教授と共に勤務していた。当時は、制がん剤や新メカニズムの医薬品は、ほぼ米国・欧州からのものであった。私もPMDAを訪ねたり、当時の築地の国立がんセンターを訪ねたりしていた。昨年(2019年)10年余務めた近藤前理事長が退任し、次は誰なのか厚労省に尋ねてみた。ところが、東京でも京都でもない、でも国立大だよという。ハハーン、それを誇りに思っており、頭がよくジェニアス(genius)な人がいる。それが、藤原康弘現PMDA理事長である。

*Yasuhiro Fujiwara*
藤原康弘

前置きが長くなった。藤原氏がPMDA理事長を引き受ける時に、「患者満足度の向上」を宣言している。理論と同時に実践派(現場主義)なのである。多分、いろんな場所を訪ねているのではないかと思う。相手も驚きますね、そして他人(ひと)が魅了される。東大病院の元病院長が、「彼は、すごく頭がいい！」と感心しきりであった。それもその筈である。

Narrative 30

# An SOS to PMDA Chief Executive Yasuhiro Fujiwara

I have briefly touched upon, within Narrative 29, the period when I was the Technical Representative for the Pharmaceutical Research Manufacturers Association (PhRMA, Washington D.C.), the current Chief Executive of the PMDA (Pharmaceuticals and Medical Devices Agency) Mr. Fujiwara was representing the Japanese Association of Medical Sciences (President Fumimaro Takaku) working with Professor Kazuhiro Sase of Juntendo University. At the time, the majority of anticancer drugs or new mechanism drugs, were from the U.S. or Europe. I, myself, would make visits to the PMDA as well as, the National Cancer Center of Japan, in Tsukiji. Last year (2019), former Chief Executive Kondo, retiring after a tenure of more than a decade, I asked the Ministry of Health, Labor and Welfare (MHLW) as to who would be next. Whereas, the response was not from Tokyo or Kyoto, but a national university. Ah, well I thought with pride, that is where there are those who are intelligent and within this group of individuals, there are geniuses. As with the current Chief Executive of the PMDA, Yasuhiro Fujiwara.

The foreword became long. When Mr. Fujiwara accepted the position of PMDA Chief Executive, he declared [Improving Patient Satisfaction]. He focuses upon theory, at the same time, to the practice group (a hands-on approach). It is highly probable, I imagine, that he has visited various institutions. The individual whom he meets is also surprised, and fascinated as well. The former director of the University of Tokyo Hospital, has expressed his admiration by stating; [He is extremely smart!]. It is only natural. His father, a graduate of the Science Department of the University of Tokyo, and an authority on the theory of elementary particles,

父君は東大理学部卒の素粒子論の大家で米国ハーバード大に留学中に理事長が誕生した。帰国後、広島大学に教授として赴任。そういうわけで、藤原理事長はバイリンガルとともにバイ国籍：米国・日本でもある。

「藤原先生、SOSです」は、がん関係あるいは分からない病気について聞かれると、私が理事長に送るメールです。まあー、時には30秒、2時間以内に必ず返事が来る…どのような案件ですか、それなら何日の何時に築地のここに来てください。

とにかく疲れを知らないすごい人なのである。東京の広い庭で腕立て伏せでもしているのかな。

理事長は、国立がん（研究）センターの時から数十年にわたって、日本の患者にも内外の新薬を世界の患者と同時に提供できるよう新薬の開発の進め方を考えて、民間にも分け隔てなくアドバイスして来られた。講演でも、ニコニコしながら容赦なく自身の考えをぶっつけて平然としている。

先にも述べたが「患者満足度の向上」の実践として、「健康被害の救済」、「承認審査」と「安全対策」を改めてPMDA運営の柱にした。特に「健康被害の救済」は日本独自の項目で、米国FDAをはじめ欧米には存在しない。近藤前理事長もよく強調していたことである。日本に登記している製薬関連会社は、欧米を問わず参加している。これがPMDAの長年の伝統である。安全対策も、新しいメカニズムのバイオ医薬品が出てくると、各専門家のチームを組んで進めなくてはならないことを強調している。おそらく、合理性の強い方なので、申請者とPMDAが直接会話することなどを進めるだろう。勿論、それには暗号を取り決め、会話をする人を案件ごとに特定し、いわゆるデュー・デリジェンスのようなプロセスをするのであろう。バイオ医薬品の製造（マニュファクチャリング）も国境を越えて行われるようになり、そうした製品の品質管理も大変である。理事長のアッケラカンとした「リーダーシップ」に期待して止まない。

藤原のヤっさん、がんばってください！　若かったころの懐かしい呼び名で「時の流れは常なるを」を感じている。

while studying abroad at Harvard University in the U.S. the Chief Executive was born. After returning to Japan, he took on the post of professor at Hiroshima University. It is for this reason; Chief Executive Fujiwara is bi-lingual as well as bi-nationalities: American and Japanese. Please confirm, for if I am not mistaken, dual nationalities of American and Japanese are not possible after the age of 21 or 23.

'SOS, Dr. Fujiwara.'Is how I start an email to the Chief Executive whenever it is cancer related issue or a disease that I am not aware of. Oh, at times within 30 seconds, or 2 hours, a response would definitely come, in which he would inquire on the details of my inquiry, and depending upon the contents, would propose a meeting on a specific time/day and location within the Tsukiji area.

His stamina is amazing, he does not seem to tire at all. I wonder if he is doing push-ups in his spacious garden in Tokyo.

The Chief Executive, over his several decades at the National Cancer (research) Center, was thinking of methods to progress the development of new drugs that would allow Japanese patients, as well, access to new domestic and international drugs, simultaneously, providing non-discriminatingly advice to the private sector. Even within the lectures he gave, though always amiable, he would relentlessly express his personal thoughts and views nonchalantly.

To place in practice the aforementioned [Improving Patient Satisfaction], areas in [Health Damage Relief], [Approval Examination Process] and [Safety Measures], were renewed and established as pillars of PMDA administration. Particularly, the area of [Health Damage Relief] is distinct to Japan and does not exist in the U.S.'s Food and Drug Administration (FDA), or counterpart European agencies. Former Chief Executive Kondo also placed emphasis on this area. Pharmaceutical related corporations registered in Japan, regardless of European and American origins participate. This has been a long tradition of the PMDA. An emphasis is placed on structuring specific specialist teams when approaching safety measures, and a biopharmaceutical with new mechanisms. In all likelihood, the practicality is stronger, and direct communications between the applicant and PMDA may progress. Of course, to do so, it is likely that an establishment of a code (cryptic), the specification of the individual who will communicate on a particular matter, in short, a process similar to due diligence. The manufacturing of biopharmaceuticals is conducted over international borders, making it difficult to oversee product quality. I continue in anticipation toward the Chief Executive's happy go lucky [leadership].

Yassan Fujiwara, Good Luck! I am referring to you with the rememberable name of our youth, I feel that [Time Flows as Usual].

第31話　初出：2020年4月13日

# 永山　治――中外製薬の名誉会長になる

*Osamu Nagayama*
永山　治氏（1947年〜）

永山治氏（永山さん）との出会いも一昔前である。初めてお会いしたのは、永山さんが中外製薬の上野社長（オーナー）のご息女と結婚し長らくロンドン勤務の後、中外製薬に入社された頃、おそらく1980年前後である。当時私は、石油に見切りをつけた三菱油化にバイオ医薬品の開発を任せるからと請われ大学から転職していた。三菱油化は中外製薬に医薬品を販売委託していた関係で、中外の上野社長が永山さんに私と会うことを薦めてくれたのだろうか、帝国ホテルのロビーでお会いしたのを覚えている。その後、中外の社長、会長を務める傍ら、また若くして（51歳）1998年製薬協の会長に就任、3期6年間務められて業界の交通整理、政府関係とのパイプ作り、バイオ関係も含め遺憾なくリーダーシップを発揮された。世間でよく知られた事実であり、筆者が触れることでもないと思われる。そしてエリスロポエチンで培ったバイオセンターを世界トップになるまで投資を続けたのは、これまたお見事。

エリスロポエチンと言えば、中外・アップジョンの製品名マローゲン（marogen）を中外が販売していたが、中外が1990年ジェネティクス・インスティチュート社と共同開発したエリスロポエチンを発売した。それを知ったアップジョン社のCEOテッド・クーパー（Dr. Ted Cooper、

Narrative31

# Osamu Nagayama Becomes Honorary Chairman of Chugai Pharmaceutical Co., Ltd.

It is quite some time ago that I met Mr. Osama Nagayama. Our first meeting occurred when Nagayama-san had married the daughter of Chugai Pharmaceutical's president Ueno (owner of the firm), and after working for an extended period in London, joined Chugai Pharmaceutical, which would be before or after 1980. At the time, I had received, and accepted, an offer from Mitsubishi Petrochemical Co., Ltd., which was abandoning oil, to oversee the development of biopharmaceuticals, resulting my departure from the University. Since Mitsubishi Petrochemical was commissioning the sales of pharmaceuticals to Chugai Pharmaceutical, president Ueno of Chugai, in all likelihood, arranged a meeting between Nagayama-san and myself, I recall that we met in the Imperial Hotel lobby. After which, while serving as president and chairman of Chugai, although still relatively young (51 years old), in 1998, he was appointed as chairman of the Japan Pharmaceutical Manufacturers Association (JPMA), a position he retained for 3 terms, 6 years, in which he conduct industry coordination, establishing channels with government related individuals, and including bio related matters, demonstrated the utmost leadership. An accomplish that is widely known to the public, and a fact that does not need me to touch upon. His steadfast investment toward creating one of the world's top bio centers, cultivated by Erythropoietin, was truly amazing.

Speaking of Erythropoietin, although Chugai Upjohn's product named marogen was being sold by Chugai, in 1990, Chugai co-developed with Genetics Institute Inc. Erythropoietin which it marketed. Upon learning this, Upjohn CEO Dr. Ted Cooper (former Assistant Secretary of Department of Education and Director of Cornell University Medical College) was enraged, which, at this stage is a fond old memory. At the time I was employed by Upjohn, and was the particular recipient of Dr. Cooper's kindness. I believe Chugai Upjohn's Nagayama-san experienced the same. Dr. Cooper was relatively small in stature, commuting to work, he would not use the corporate car but would drive his own four-wheel drive vehicle which had a higher driver's seat. At least while commuting, he could look down on people. However, he was also fond of people of small stature.

Nagayama-san utilizing his English language capabilities, polished during his tenure in

教育省次官、コーネル大医学部長など歴任）の激怒も、今となっては懐しい思い出である。当時アップジョン社に奉職していたので、Dr. クーパーには特別に可愛がってもらった。中外・アップジョンの永山さんも同じだったと思う。Dr. クーパーは小柄で、通勤に会社の専用車でなく運転席の高い四輪駆動車を運転していた。運転のときくらいは見下ろしたかったのである。しかし小柄な人が好みでもあった。

永山さんは、ロンドンでポリッシュした英語を活用し世界のロシュに乗り込み、中外という名称を残しロシュの役員におさまったのは凄いことである。名も残し実も取った離れ業で背負い投げ一本。中外（チュウガイ）という発音も響きがよいが、「なか」と「そと」という漢字も創業者の強い意志が読み取れる。

また永山さんは、2013年度には東京大学経済学部の「産業事情」講座で講義をしている。それが、「新産業論」に発展したのかとも思われる。永山さんが語る製薬業界の懸案事項である薬価制度について同感なので触れたいと思う。何せ日本の製薬産業は規模が小さいので、内を向かずに外を向いている。臨床研究も外で行う傾向がある。薬価が高い米国を睨んでいる。米国には公的薬価はなく、企業の希望価格が存在する。トランプ大統領も院内・院外とも、50％減を指示している。日本ももはや希望価格を薬価とは取らないであろう。米国にある公認のロビイスト制度も必要だ。政治家がロビイストの役をやるのはいかがなものか。

さて、中外製薬の評判がすこぶる良いことは株価にも表れている。永山さんの手腕はもちろんであるが、その政策を真剣に自ら考え実行し、永山さんの後を継いで新会長に就任された小坂達朗CEOや奥田修新社長、上野幹夫副会長など役員の方々、さらに汗を流している従業員の皆さんの役割も大きい。企業には浮き沈みはつきものであるが、永山さんがいれば大丈夫。

London, boldly visited the global Roche, and negotiated retaining the Chugai name as well as a place at the board of directors, was masterful. Keeping the name, and taking the fruit as well, is one decisive Seoi throw (judo). The pronunciation of Chugai, possesses a good resonance, however it is the characters utilized in the name Chu (within) and Gai (outside), that one can comprehend the strong convictions of the founders.

In addition, Nagayama-san had provided a lecture to the Faculty of Economics of the University of Tokyo, on [The Status of Industry] in 2013. This has, I believe, has developed into [New Industry Debates]. A pending issue within the pharmaceutical industry, that Nagayama-san speaks of, is the drug pricing system, which I concur with and will like to touch upon. At any rate, in view that the size of Japan's pharmaceutical industry is small, it is not looking within, but facing outwardly. The trend has become to conducting clinical research abroad. Glaring at the U.S. where the prices of pharmaceuticals are high. The United States do not have a public drug pricing system, what exists is that corporations can price their own products. Even President Trump has directed that, in and out, hospital dispensary makes a reduction in prices by 50%. Alas, Japan will be no longer be able to get a manufacturer recommended price in drug prices. As with the United States, it is also necessary to have a certified lobbyist system. Having politicians playing the part of lobbyist is somewhat dubious.

Well, the reputation of Chugai Pharmaceuticals is extremely good, as can be seen in its stock prices. There is no doubt of Nagayama-san's ability, but it was his approach to policy; placing his own serious thoughts to, and placing this into practice. Following after Nagayama-san, appointed as the new chairman Mr. Tatsuro Kosaka and new president Mr. Osamu Okuda, as well as the directors such as, vice-chairman Mr. Mikio Ueno, a not to mention the employees; who will experience further exert in efforts, everyone has vital roles to play. Corporations always experience ups and downs, however if Nagayama-san is there, it will be alright.

第32話　　初出：2020年4月27日

# 熱中症から救ってくれた老年内科医——小川 純人

*Sumito Ogawa*
小川純人

小川純人東大准教授（老年病学）と知り合いになった切っ掛けは、小川先生の奥様の母君が、女子英語会を主催しておられるので、その仲間の話し（英語）を聞いてほしいという筆者の友人である布施敏夫さんからの依頼でありました。喜んでお受けした2018年6月11日昼頃、9名の仲間と来られ各自が経歴を英語で話されました。そして私がコメントと言いますか、感想を述べるという実に楽しい一時（いっとき／一時間半）を過ごしたのです。良い思い出になりました。

そして猛暑の同年7月20日、熱中症を心配した息子が東大病院の老年病学科に直接電話をして、東大病院に緊急入院し一週間お世話になり26日に無事退院いたしました。まさに命を救われた感じでした。心からの鳴謝です。その時の主治医が、小川先生であったのは、なおさら幸運でした。

先生はまさに人格者で、旧海軍兵学校ではありませんが、まさに五省の方である。言行不一致はなかったか、気力は十分か、などなど……。

さて小川先生の老年病関連領域での活躍は、ある調査会社のアンケート結果によると、聞きたい講演の演者No.1は小川先生であったことを見ても分かります。先生の研究について述べたいと思います。2001年から2005年にかけてカリフォルニア大学サンディエゴ校（UCSD）に留

Narrative32

# Dr. Sumito Ogawa, a Geriatrics Specialist Who Saved Me from Heatstroke

*Prof. Ogawa's students*

The background of my meeting with Sumito Oagawa, associate professor, University of Tokyo was, his wife's mother held an English conversation group for women, and I had received a request from my friend Toshio Fuse-san, to listen to these ladies speaking in English. I was more than happy to accept, and on June 11th, 2018, around noon, accompanied with nine of her group, she made the visit to my office, where each member relayed their individual backgrounds in English. I was to make comments and convey my impressions, it was a truly enjoyable time (an hour and half), spent. It has become a good memory.

On an exceptionally hot day of July 20th of the same year, concerned that I was suffering from heatstroke, my son made a direct phone call to the department of Geriatrics of the University of Tokyo Hospital, which resulted in an immediate admission, where I stayed for a week, being discharged on the 26th. I felt that my life was saved. I am deeply grateful. The attending physician was Dr. Ogawa, an added good fortune.

The doctor is an individual of character, although not of the former naval academy, he reflects the five admonitions, or counsel introduced by this institution. The absence of any inconsistency between words and actions, adequacy in vigor, etc. etc.

Now, the scope of Dr. Ogawa's geriatrics related achievements is starkly evident in the results of a research firm's questionnaire, in which the question was asked; "Whose lecture would you like listen to?" Dr. Ogawa came in as Number 1. I would like to touch upon what Dr. Ogawa's research. From 2001 to 2005, he was studying at the University of California San Diego. To concentrate on his research, he pursued this time abroad leaving his family in Japan. Outstanding! My personal view is [What a wasted opportunity.] He could have taken his family with him.

To begin with, during his university years, he studied in the Reproductive, Developmen-

学されています。研究に没頭するため単身赴任だったというから、お見事！　筆者から見ると、「もったいない」―― なぜご家族を連れて行かなかったのと。

まず、大学院時代（東京大学大学院医学系研究科生殖・発達・加齢医学専攻）は、老年における性ホルモンの役割について基礎研究を行い、結果、エストリジェン受容体を改変したトランスジェニックラットを作成しエストロゲンの骨作用について解明されました（J Bio Chem 2000）。

そして、カリフォルニア大学サンディエゴ校となるわけですが、細胞分子医学教室（Department of Cellular and Molecular Medicine）のChristopher K. Glass教授の指導の下、ステロイド受容体などの抗炎症作用を解明しています。成果は、Proc Natl Acad Sci USA 2004、Cell 2005、Nat Rev Immunol 2006、Mol Cell 2020に公開されています。

帰国後は、老年疾患の病態解明やホルモンとの関連性について基礎・臨床研究を進めているといい、成果はOsteoporosis Int 2019、Geriatr Geron Int 2019、J Bone Minaer Metab 2020、Dysphagia 2020に発表されています。

最後になりますが、小川先生によりますと老年医学の問題は、老年疾患の発生機序、治療・予防法の解明といった臨床的課題と老化の本質・制御といった基礎的課題に大別されますが、両課題に対しての研究を継続、発展していきたい、そのためにも、医薬連携や老年学、AIの活用など、健康寿命延伸に向けた学際的研究を一層推進したいと言っておられます。

また私ごとですが、とある検査のため去る3月10日から13日まで東大病院消化器内科に入院しました。全身麻酔でしたので、小川先生には入院時また退院時にもお越しいただき病状確認をしていただきました。改めて深謝でございます。小川先生の益々のご発展と成功を祈念してお開きとしたい。

tal and Aging Science Course of the University of Tokyo, Graduate School of Medicine, in which he pursued fundamental research into the functions of hormones in aging, resulting in identifying the bone reaction made by the estrogen of a transgenic rat with an altered estrogen receptor (J Bio Chem 2000).

This leads to the University of California San Diego, under the guidance of Professor Christopher K. Glass, of the Department of Cellular and Molecular Medicine, where clarifies anti-inflammatory effects of steroid receptors. Results are made public within; Proc Nat Acad Sci USA 2004, Cell 2005, Nat Rev Immunol 2006, MolCell 2020.

Upon returning to Japan, he continued to conduct, basic and clinical research into geriatric disease, as well as the relationship of hormones, results are published within; Osteoporosis Int2019, Geriatr Geron Int 2019, J Bone Minaer Metab 2020, Dysphagia 2020.

Last but not least, according to Dr. Ogawa, the issue of geriatrics can be broadly classified into; solving the clinical issues into the mechanism of occurrence, treatment/prevention, and the fundamental issues into the true essence/control over aging, he states that he would like to continue research and make develops to both issues, to accomplish this, he notes the cooperation of the pharmaceutical sector, gerontology, the utilization of AI, etc. and the further promotion of interdisciplinary research toward extending the healthy life expectancy.

On a personal note, last March 10th to the 13th, I was admitted to the Gastroenterology Department of the University of Tokyo Hospital for a test. As the test required general anesthesia, I requested Dr. Ogawa to be present during my admission and discharge to conduct a confirmation of the condition. I would again like to express my deepest gratitude. I pray for Dr. Ogawa's continued progress and success.

## 第33話

初出：2020年5月25日

# 木から滑っても、なお男
# ——ウォーレン・バフェット

© Sipa USA/amanaimages

*Warren Buffett*
ウォーレン・バフェット（1930～）

……野球の神様もたまには三振、エラーもする……これは灰田勝彦の「野球小僧」の歌詞の一節で、たまに負けても選手は動じない（素心）ということである。神様バフェット氏も、たまにはエラーもするという話（アマゾン株、後述）。

バフェット氏も、たまに失敗をしても、神様であり（レジェンド／Legend）・カリスマ（Charisma）でもあることに変わりはない。次の事例が如実に物語っている。例年どおり昨年も、バフェット氏と昼食（NYの有名ステーキ・ハウス）をする権利を慈善オークションで募ったところ殺到した中で権利を得たのは…。

匿名とされていたが、何とジャスティン・サン（Justin Sun）である。仮想通貨「トロン」の創設者で、中国生まれ（1990年）、北京大学卒業のハイ・テックの最先端を行く凄い青年である（今年30歳）。落札額の公表無しと言われてきたが、彼は平気でしゃべり、457万ドル（約5億円）であるという。2012年、2016年に記録した約350万ドル（約3.8億円）を抜く過去最高額だ。この辺が、彼の素早い所であるが、何が狙いなのか。

## Narrative 33

# Even Slipping from a Tree, the Man, Warren Buffet, Founder of Berkshire Hathaway

A legendary professional ballplayer may, at times, strike out, or make mistakes, this is a lyric from Katsuhiko Haida's song [the Baseball Kid], it goes on to say that, if the game is lost, players are not shaken (soshin). This narrative is about how, similarly, the legendary Mr. Buffett, at times, has made mistakes (Amazon stocks, later in the text).

Mr. Buffett, although may make mistakes, his legendary status and charisma, does not change. The following example vividly reflects this. As usual, as it was last year, the right to lunch with Mr. Buffett (at New York's famous steak house) was gathered through a charity auction site which was flooded with those who wishing to the right, in this overwhelming attraction, just who won....

Although it was to be anonymous, it was Justin Sun. He is the founder of the cryptocurrency platform [TRON], was born in China in 1990, graduating from Peking University, is a highly successful young (30 years old this year) cutting-edge tech entrepreneur. What was supposed to be an undisclosed successful bid amount, he openly stated that it was 4.57 million dollars (roughly 500 million yen). Overtaking the highest recorded bid of 2012 and 2016, which was approximately 3.5 million dollars (roughly 380 million yen), making his bid the highest ever recorded. This is where his quickness is evident, but what was his aim?

Getting back to the main subject. It is of Mr. Buffett, the legendary fund investor, chairman and CEO of the investment/insurance firm, Berkshire Hathaway (at the end of 2018 had invested $173 billion/approximately 19 trillion yen, a world class top sum), a narrative on, who

さて本論に戻そう。投資ファンドの神様で、投資・保険会社バークシャー・ハサウェイ（Berkshire Hathaway、2018年末で＄173bn／約19兆円というのは世界トップクラスの投資額である）を運営しているバフェット氏ですら、たまにはエラーもすることがあるという話。氏は、アマゾン株の買いも遅かったが、売りのタイミングの遅れも認めて、今回は負けたねと認めたという（平常心）。しかし、氏はアマゾン創業者のベゾス氏（Bezos）とは親友で、アマゾン株を買わないなんてお馬鹿さん（idiot）だねと自身思っていたという。この辺が、バフェット氏の心意気である。友情のためなら、損は覚悟の上だ（思いやり／empathy）。

バフェット氏は54年の投資生活の中で、面白いことにヨーロッパに興味がなく、もっぱら米国内に投資してきた。最初は金融や消費財（コカ・コーラ）に中心を置いてきたが、2011年に初めてIT分野に進出しIBMに投資、続いてアップルと…。思うに、氏の直轄部下である左・右の両腕（TCとTW）がIT分野のスピード感に後れを取ったのではないかと思う。これが米国のカッティング・スロート（cutting throat／生き馬の目を抜く）の世界である。

バフェット氏の投資スタイルは、いわゆるバイ・アンド・ホールドで、相場の暴落時に成長する見込みのある安い株を買って、値上がりを待ち長期保有をするというバフェット法則である。

また、彼の名を冠したBuffett's Alphaという言葉がメディアで見かけるようになった。バフェット氏は投資に対するリスクがシャープ・レシオ（ノーベル経済学賞受賞者W. F. Sharpeの創生）が、0.79ならよいとして投資を続けてきた、2013年以来。おそらく、これからもこの線を崩さず行くのだろう。2018年末で、バフェット氏（バークシャー）のアップルを含めた投資総額は＄173bnである。バフェット氏は今年で90歳になる、そしてメディア王マードック氏も89歳だ。しかも健康で、頭も冴えているとくりゃー、いうことなし。益々のご健勝とご発展を祈りたい。見習いたいものである。

at times, also makes errors. Although he was late in accumulating Amazon shares, his timing of elling off was also late, he calmly admitted defeat. He and Amazon founder Mr. Bezos are good friends, and he himself said he was an idiot not to have bought Amazon shares. This reflects the spirit of Mr. Buffet. For the sake of friendship, he is prepared to accept a loss, he is considerate and possesses empathy.

Within Mr. Buffett's 54 years of investment activities, it is interesting to note that he is not interested in Europe, focusing purely on investments within the United States. Although initially centralizing on finances and consumer products (Coca Cola), in 2011, for the first time he progressed into the IT sector, investing in IBM and on to Apple. I presume that his direct subordinates; left and right arms, (TC and TW) were late in recognizing the speed of the IT sector. This is America's cutthroat business world.

Mr. Buffett's investment style is, what can be referred as, buy and hold. When the market price falls, he will buy stocks cheaply of firms in which there is potential for growth, keeping these stocks while waiting for the prices to rise is the Buffett rule.

Also taking his name, there is a phrase referred to as Buffett's Alpha, that can be seen in the media. William F. Sharpe, creator of the Sharpe ratio and winner of the Nobel Prize in Economics, reflects on Mr. Buffet's investments and says that if it is 0.79 he will continue to invest, which he has done since 2013. It is highly that this string of thought will not give way. At the end of 2018, Mr. Buffett's (Berkshire) investment total, including Apple, was $173 billion. This year, Mr. Buffett will become 90 years old, and the media mogul Murdoch will be 89 years old. Healthy, as well as, possessing a clear, brilliant mind, what more could you want. I continue to pray for his health and progress. I would like to follow his example.

第34話　　初出：2020年6月8日

# 高校・大学の畏敬の先輩
# ――海老原昭夫

高校、大学の先輩である海老原昭夫氏は東大医学部を卒業後、東大上田内科に入局し2年の後、テキサス大学に留学し(1年半)、インディアナ大学に移り2年半を臨床薬理学を極めるために費やした。しかし、その前に米国で臨床を進めるためには米国での医師免許が不可欠である。

そのために、外国人用の医師免許(ESMA)まで取得するという努力を惜しまなかった。これは、大変な仕事であると同時に不屈の精神が必要である。我らが母校である高校の校歌にある「むかーし、天下を睥睨の東男(あずまおとこ)の魂はこの三寸の胸にあり」の精神がこれを成し遂げさせたのである。帰国後、大分医科大学医学部教授となり、日本での最初の臨床薬理学講座を立ち上げた。大分で9年を過ごし、自治医科大学医学部教授(臨床薬理学)に移った。医学の研究と教育に多大な貢献をされた先生である。

ご家族は、ご長男、次男、お嬢さんもお医者さんという、まさに、医師一家である。

さて、後輩として先輩の人間に触れたいと思う。先輩は、茨城県水海

Narrative 34

# Akio Ebihara, My Revered High School and University Senior

A senior of my high school and university, Mr. Akio Ebihara, after graduating from the Faculty of Medicine, of the University of Tokyo, entered University of Tokyo's Ueda Internal Medicine, and after 2 years, went to study at the University of Texas (a year and a half), moving on to the University of Indiana committing himself to a further 2 years and a half to the studies of clinical pharmacology. However, prior to this, it is absolutely necessary to obtain a medical license in the U.S. to proceed with his clinical studies.

For this, he did not spare the efforts in applying for a medical license for non-Americans. This is an extremely arduous process that requires unyielding determination. Our school song has the lyrics to the effect, [Glare at the world to express the force of your influence, the eastern man's (this reference to eastern man, divides Japan between east and west) spirit is within one's chest] this spirit, in all likelihood, led to his accomplishments. Upon returning to Japan, he became a professor at the Faculty of Medicine, Oita Medical College, establishing Japan's first course in clinical pharmacology. Living in Oita for 9 years, he transferred to professorship at Faculty of Medicine (clinical pharmacology), Local Autonomy College. This was followed by recognizing his immense contribution to the research of medicine and education.

His family, two sons and a daughter are all physicians, truly a family of physicians.

Well, as his junior, I would like to touch upon my senior. My senior was born near Mitsukaido city of Ibaragi Prefecture, after old education system Mitsukaido Junior High School, he went on to study and graduate in the new-education-system Mitsukaido High School (one-year absence due to illness). Passing the entrance examination on the first attempt, he was accepted to Natural Sciences II, of the University of Tokyo. At the time when he announced [I want to take the entrance exams for the University of Tokyo] to his then high school Principle Komatsu responded [You will not pass, if you do pass, come to me], when he did pass, he reported [I passed] the principle's response was, [Young man, it is not right to lie. You would not have passed. Bring your student's identification card and come again.]. Well, it was a delightful period, a really funny story. However, this Principle Komatsu, when my senior entered old education system Mitsukaido Junior High School, made special efforts to allow him to be the

道(みつかいどう)市の近郊に生まれ、旧制水海道中学を経て新制水海道第一高等学校(1年病欠)を卒業した。そして東大理科2類に現役合格した。当時の小松校長に「東大を受験したい」というと、「お前に受かる筈がない、合格したら来い」と言われ、「合格しました」と言ったら、「君、うそを言ってはいけない。合格する筈がない。学生証を持って、もう一度来い」と言われたという。まあー、何とも愉快な時代であり、おもろい話である。しかし、小松校長は、先輩が旧制水海道中学に入学したとき、大学まで続く奨学金を受けられるように取り計らってくれたという。成績が良かったからに違いない。また先輩の母君は、当時の東大病院で看護婦兼産婆(現・助産師)をなされていた。

つい最近電話で話をした時、茨城弁丸出しで「小林君よー、人間には誰にでもよー、ヒョウタンから駒ってことがあるんだよなー、うーん」と言う。なんとも言いようのない良き先輩である。

私にとってのヒョウタンから駒は、いつだったのかなあー。高卒後、他大学の医学部には合格し1年ほど通ったが、翌年東大理科2類に合格した。医者にはならなかったが、先輩とは大学でも似た道を歩んだ。先輩は東大医学部医学科に進学し、私は東大医学部薬学科に進学した。こうして薬学を選んだということがなければ、今の私「専門は再生医療・文筆家で2冊の出版本(和文・英文)あり」とはいかなかったであろう。

しかし、私にとっての「駒」はもう一つあったような気がする。それは、1962年、オーストラリア政府による、Sirフローリーや Sirエックルスといったノーベル医学賞受賞者が2人もいたオーストラリア国立大学の医系大学院の留学生国際公募に合格したという、思いもよらぬ「駒」に出会ったことである。この「駒」がなければ、米国製薬企業トップ10のアップジョンやE.リリーのディビジョン・VPになることも無かったであろう。

先輩、スペースを私事でいただきすみません。先輩にふさわしい後輩と思ってお許しを——厚かましい。……Pardon me !

recipient of a scholarship all the way to university. There is no doubt that this special attention was due to his good grades. My senior's mother was, at the time, a nurse and midwife at the University of Tokyo Hospital.

Just recently when I phoned him, speaking in a strong Ibaragi dialect, he said [Kobayashi-kun, it can happen to anyone, it's like something appearing from a place you would least expect. A wonderful senior that anyone could have.

When was the time that I received something from a place least expected? After graduating from high school, I passed an exam for another university, where I attended for a year, the following year I passed the exam for Natural Sciences II, the University of Tokyo. Although I did not become a physician, I did proceed a similar path as my senior. My senior studied at the School of Medicine, the University of Tokyo, and I studied at the Pharmaceutical Sciences of the University of the Tokyo School of Medicine. If I had not chosen pharmaceutical sciences, I would not have been able to author 2 volumes of the published [My Specialty is Regenerative Medicine] (Japanese/English editions).

However, I feel that I have one more [something]. That is, in 1962, when I pass the examination that was offered through an open call for foreign students, conducted by the Australian government, to attend the National University of Australia, Graduate School of Medicine, from which learned Nobel prize in Medicine winners , such as, Sir Howard W. Florey and Sir John C. Eccles hailed, this was indeed something from a place least expected. If I had not received this [something], I would not have had professional careers within two of America's top 10 pharmaceutical corporations, Upjohn and Eli Lilly's Division VP.

Senior, apologies for taking up space on my own experience. I hope that you will feel that I am a junior worthy of you. Again, many apologies. Pardon me!

# 第35話

初出：2020年7月13日

# ヒスタミンロマンス ——C. Robin Ganellin

C. ロビン・ガネリン ロンドン大学名誉教授と妻モニーク

ユダヤ人であることに誇りを持ち、その民族を讃える我が親友ロビン・ガネリン（C. Robin Ganellin）が創成したのがタガメット（Tagamet）である。新薬の発見・開発の国際業界でタガメットを知らない人はいないであろう。十二指腸潰瘍が無くなり外科医が十二指腸潰瘍の手術を経験出来なくなったというくらい途轍もないブロックバスターである。その発見・開発者の1人がロビンである。このうちの1人であるジェームス W.ブラック（Sir James W. Black）教授は1988年ノーベル医学・生理学賞をほかの2人と受賞した。が、ロビンは外れた。ノーベル賞は最大3人が規定である、4人目はない。

それ以降、ロビンは国際医薬品化学の世界で大御所として尊敬される存在となり、今日まで来ている。とにかく他人（ひと）の話をよく聞き面倒見がよい。筆者がロビンと知り合ったのは、数十年前、筆者が日本学術会議を代表して国際純正・応用化学連合（IUPAC、当時は英国オックスフォード大に本部）の雑誌（Chemistry）に共著で報告した時からである。

帝政ロシア時代、彼のユダヤ系祖父母（宝石商）はウクライナに住んでいたが、帝政ロシアの悪党コサックに着の身着のまま追い出され、ファ

## Narrative 35

# Histamine Romance —— C. Robin Ganellin

C. Robin Ganellin, a good friend who is proud of his Jewish lineage, as well as praising the Jewish race, created Tagamet. Within the international pharmaceutical drug and development sector, anyone who is involved in the international drug research and development sector is aware of Tagamet. Its effectivity in illuminating duodenal ulcers is said to have denied surgeons the experience of operating on duodenal ulcers, making Tagamet a tremendous block buster. Involved in its discovery and development were three individuals, one of them being Robin. Although Professor Sir James W. Black, in 1998 was awarded the Nobel Prize in Physiology or Medicine with two other individuals, Robin was excluded. Nobel Prize rules only allow a maximum of 3 individuals to be awarded in relation to a specific shared achievement, there is no allowance for a 4th individual.

Needless to say, thereafter, Robin became a world renown influential member of the international medicinal chemistry sector, highly respected to this day. Possessing the skill to intently listen to what others are saying, as well as looking after, and offering support. I became acquainted with Robin several decades ago when as a representative of the Science Council of Japan, co-authored a report for the magazine [Chemistry] of the International Pure and Applied Chemistry/IUPAC, which at the time had its headquarters in England's Oxford University.

During the Imperial Russia period, his Jewish grandparents (jewelers) resided in Ukraine, however they were forced to flee with nothing but the clothes on their backs from the notorious Cossacks of Imperial Russia, loosing virtually all their personal belongings, including the family history. This led to the family moving to England which were accepting Jewish immigrants from Ukraine. It was at this time that they were instructed to change their names to adaptable to English, thus his grandfather became Harris Ganelin. However, he made an error in his spelling, becoming Harris Ganellin, the double ll is how it is spelled to this day. The [C] of C.Robin Ganellin has a story in itself. Charon was taken from Greek mythology, he was born on January 25th as the first boy, and although his uncle stressed that Reuben, which means the first-born boy would be appropriate, he was named a notably English name Robin.

ミリー・ヒストリーを含むすべての私物を失った。そして、ウクライナのユダヤ人を移民として受け入れた英国に移り住んだ。その時、名前を英国風に変えるように指示があり祖父はハリス・ガネリン（Harris Ganelin）となった。が、担当者が書き間違いHarris Ganellinとなり、そのまま今日まで来ているという。C. Robin GanellinのC.にも一言あるという。Charonはギリシャ神話からきているが、ロビンは、伯父さんの口添えもあり、長男として1月25日に誕生したのだから、長男を意味するReubenであると主張し、英語風のRobinとなったのだという。そして天に向かって"Robin、Robin、Robin …"と叫んだという。とにかく、"No give up"なのだ、この男は。

そして、ロビンのジュニア・ハイやハイスクール時の活動は、Independent thinker（物まねはしない）そのもので、サイクリング・クラブに大人に混じって1日走っていた。学校はスッポカシ…といった有様、海釣りと川釣りと、まあー「悪ガキ」そのものであった。

しかし、いよいよ大学を考える時がくると、一変！　猛勉強開始。オックスフォード大学の経済学部に入学したが、どうも性に合わない。有機合成化学に転向し、博士号D. Phil（グラスゴウ大もD. Phil）を取得。ケンブリッジ大他（東大も）博士号としてPH. D. を使う。とにかく外柔内剛で、実に頭のよい天才肌の男である。第二次世界大戦中、分析化学者の父親（Leon Ganellin）は家族をウクライナに残してロンドンの分析化学者のドクター・バーナードの会社で働いていた。英国では、ウクライナ時代の初恋のタマラ（Tamara）と結婚（1956年）。ロンドンのUCLで学びフランス語の教師だった彼女は、脳腫瘍にて他界した（1997年）。そしてヒスタミン研究を介してフランスの研究機関（CNRS）の薬理学者だったモニーク（Monique Garbarg、Ph. D. ）と結ばれたのは2003年6月である。彼は、ヒスタミン・ロマンスという。日本とも関わりがあり、2度来日している。

Voices were raised to heaven, “Robin, Robin, Robin . . . .” This man is a “Never give up” type of individual.

The activities that Robin pursued during his junior high and high school years reflects his nature as a true independent thinker (an individual who does not copy what others do), joining adults of a cycling club, to ride about throughout the day, ultimately skipping school, and enjoying sea and river fishing, he was a truly [naughty boy].

However, when it was time to think of college, the change was immediate. He studied with immense fervor. He was accepted to the department of economics of Oxford University, which he felt out of line with. Transferring to Synthetic Organic Chemistry, ultimately acquiring a D. Phil (and a D. Phil from the University of Glasgow). At Cambridge University, among others, (including the University of Tokyo) the doctorate degree is represented as Ph.D. Possessing a gentle appearance masking a formidable will, and a brilliant mind. During the Second World War, his father Leon Ganellin, who was an analytic chemist, left his family in Ukraine to move to London to work for the analytic chemistry firm of Dr. Bernard.

There is a relation to Japan as well, which he has visited twice. In March of 1984, he was the Plenary Lecturer at the General Conference of the Pharmaceutical Society of Japan, which was held in Sendai. Taking the opportunity to visit Tokyo, Kyoto and Okayama. This visit was followed by an invitation in 2000 to the international conference ‘Histamine Research in The New Millennium’, also held in Sendai, where he arrived with the Histamine Romance’s Monique.

# 第36話

初出：2020年7月27日

# Merck and Company Inc を救った男 ——K.C.フレージャー

© ZUMA Press/amanaimages

*Kenneth C.Frazier*
K.C.フレージャー

米国メルク社のCEO、COO、取締役会議長であるK.C.フレージャー（Kenneth C. Frazier、フレージャー氏）は、アフリカ系米国人として1954年に誕生（Philadelphia）、現在65歳である。父親のオチス（Otis）はビルの管理人だった。フレージャー氏が12歳の時に母親が亡くなり、寂しい思いをした。しかし、頭が良く「オタマジャクシ」や「ヤモリ」を育て、店に卸して小遣い稼ぎをしている。有名な中学・高校（モットーが「Dare to be excellent」）に入学、成績抜群で卒業。当時、フレージャー氏が憧れていたのは、最初のアフリカ系米国人で最高裁準判事を務めたサーグード・マーシャル（Thurgood Marshall、1908年〜1993年）だったという。そしてペンシルベニア州立大を経て、ハーバード大のロー・スクールをDJ（法学博士）の称号を得て卒業している。秀才中の秀才であった。それでも、尊敬する人（上記）をみると、それなりに少年時代には悔しい思いをしていたのだろうと思う。

そして法律事務所（Drinker Biddle & Reath）に就職。米国メルク社（米国以外では、MSDが使われる、日本でも）は、フレージャー氏のクライアントであったが、1992年に業務担当として入社、1999年には、上級ジェネラル・カウンセルに昇格。時に、実力発揮の事態が起こる。抗炎症剤

Narrative 36

# K.C. Frazier, the Man Who Saved Merck and Company Inc

Mr. K.(Kenneth) C. Frazier, CEO, COO and Chairperson of the Board of Directors of the American pharmaceutical firm, Merck, is a 65-year-old African-American who was born in 1954 in Philadelphia. His father Otis, was a building manager. At the age of 12, Mr. Frazier's mother passed away, was 12 years old, his mother passed away, causing the boy to experience a sense of loneliness. However, being intelligent, he would raise [tadpoles] and [geckos] which he would supply to stores to earn his allowance. Accepted to a prestigious junior and high school, whose motto is [Dare to be excellent], where he excelled and graduated with outstanding grades. At the time, Mr. Frazier's inspiration was Thurgood Marshall, (1908-1993), the first African-American to serve as Associate Justice of the Supreme Court of the United States. After studying at the Pennsylvania State University, he went on to study at Harvard Law School receiving a D.Jur. doctor's degree in law. He was the best among the best. Even with these accomplishments, when reflecting on the individual he respected (noted above), it is easy to imagine that there were times, in his boyhood, that he experienced moments of frustration.

*Tony Alvarez*
トニー・アルバレス

He was employed by the law firm of Drinker Biddle & Reath. A case in which he worked on with the two attorneys was that which won the acquittal in 1995 for "Bo" Cochran, a condemned African-American man who had been jailed for 19 years facing the death sentence for a crime he did not commit. Overnight he entered the elite group of famous attorneys. Among Mr. Frazier's clients was the America's pharmaceutical giant, Merck (known outside of the U.S., as well as Japan, as MSD). In 1992 he joined Merck in the capacity of general counsel, and in 1999 rising to become senior general counsel for the firm. The time arrived with an event that

“Vioxx”の副作用問題（心臓発作と心筋梗塞）が起こり、その対策の指揮を執ることになったのである。当時（1997年）、メディアでは＄20bnから＄50bn位が補償にかかるだろうと言われていたが、実際には、＄4.85bnにて解決を見た。それは、フレージャー氏が一括補償でなくて、個別面談を被害者と被害者の弁護士とメルク社の弁護士の三者会談を通じて個別に時間を掛けて丁寧に進めた結果だったのである。これをもって、すでに取締役社長になっていたが（2010年）、2011年1月1日にCEO、COO、取締役会議長に上り詰めた。

このような彼の人生を見て来ると、米国大統領もターゲットに入ってくるのではないかと期待が膨らむ。トランプ後は、現在62歳のニューヨーク州知事クオモ氏が本命であろうが。クオモ氏が2期（民主党）やっても、フレージャー氏はまだ72〜3歳である。十分やれる年齢である。メルク社では一昔前、社長のロイ・ヴァジロス氏（Roy Vagelos）を大統領選に、共和党が担ごうとした時があった。彼の著書『Medicine、Science and Merck』のサイン入りを、筆者はもらっている。

フレージャー氏に話を戻そう。メルク社のトップになって10年。さらに10年は続けるだろうから20年の統治になり、この辺で退任する。するとちょうどクオモ後の大統領選に間に合うことになる。乞う、ご期待！

MSDジャパンで忘れられない男が、もう一人いる。我がアップジョン時代からの親友トニー・アルバレス（Tony Alvarez）である。氏はコロンビア国出身でニュージャージー州立薬科大学を卒業しアップジョン社にメジカル・リップとして入社。日本では、MSDジャパンの代表として活躍。この業界（日本）で、「トニーを知らない人はいない、トニーが知らない人もいない」と言われた男である。良くおしゃべりし食事を楽しんだものである。今は、メルクを退職したが、旧交を温めたいものである。

would allow him to display his capabilities. Claims of side effects (heart attacks) connected to the anti-inflammatory drug "Vioxx" arose. Taking the lead and overseeing the measures to be taken. At the time, 1997, although the media were reporting compensations would amount to $20bn to $50bn, in actuality, settlements were met at $4.85bn. This is attributed to Mr. Frazier's decision to avoid a quick one-off settlement and fight each case in court, through a process of holding three party individual meetings, involving each claimant, their attorneys and attorneys of Merck, which, although time consuming was a careful and thoughtful process that brought about this settlement result. The handling of the event brought about Mr. Frazier, who was president of Merck from 2019, was further ascend to be appointed CEO, COO on January 1, 2011.

Looking at his achievements and life, hopes expand toward placing a target on a United States presidency. Post Trump, New York state governor Cuomo, who is the same age, 65, may be a favored choice. Even if Mr. Cuomo (Democratic) was to serve two terms, he would be 72-3 years old. An age that is still viable to lead. Although it is not clear as to whether Mr. Frazier is Democratic or Republican in political preference. Quite some time ago, the Republican Party had intentions to back Merck's president Roy Vergelos, as their candidate for the U.S. presidency. Since it was not a grassroot backed candidacy, the funds necessary was astronomical, I recall that the result was [... its, its impossible]. I am the owner of a signed copy of his book; [Medicine, Science and Merck]. Returning to Mr. Frazier. It has been 10 years since he has become the top of Merck. There is a continuity of a further 10 years, which would mean governing the firm for20 years, to avoid the proverbial 'getting stuck in a rut', thoughts toward a resignation may surface at around this time. This may fit into the timing of considering entering the race for the U.S. presidency post Cuomo. Stay tuned!

There is another man, within MSD Japan, that cannot be forgotten. That man is a great friend from my days at Upjohn, Tony Arbares. He hails from the South American nation, Columbia, who had immigrated to the United States. Graduating from New Jersey state pharmaceutical college and joining Upjohn as a medical rep. In Japan, he was active the leader of MSD Japan. In the pharmaceutical industry sector, he was a man described in the phrase; [There is no one who does not know Tony, and there is no one Tony does not know]. Many a time, we enjoyed meals and conversations together. Although he had resigned from Merck, I look forward to the day that we can re-visit and renew our friendship.

第37話　　初出：2020年8月11日

# アサシス社創業者

## ――CEO（Gil）、CSO（John）、COO（BJ-）そしてSVP（Manal）

*Gil Van Bokkelen*
ギル・ヴァン・ボッケレン

*John Harrington,PhD*

*William(B.J.)Lehmann,JD*

*Laura Campbell*

創業者ギル・ヴァン・ボッケレン（Gil Van Bokkelen）と初めて接点があったのは、駐日米国大使であったキャロライン・ブーヴィエ・ケネディ（Caroline Bouvier Kennedy）が離任する2017年7月4日米国独立記念日であった。旧知のウーリッヒ・タグリーバー氏（米国メルク社元VP）から前日メールがあり「明日の晩、米国から電話を日本時間の21時（9PM）に掛けるので、東大のオフィスに居てほしい」と言われた。ウーリッヒがメルク社退職後、アサシス社顧問とは驚きであった。ケネディ大使の米国大使館での離任パーティから戻ると、案の定9時きっかりに電話が来て、アサシス社の7～8人から自己紹介があり、13問の質問を受けた。が、すべてに明快な返答と彼らが理解できるよう例を挙げて説明をしてあげた。そうして、電話会議を毎週火曜日に行うようになり、マナル（Manal Morsy、元メルク社、国際規制の専門家）が、前日アジェンダをメールしてくる習慣となった。そのうち、電話はコストがかかるので、メールによる質疑応答となる。2017年よりアドバイザーをしていたので、アサシス社のミッションが来ると、厚労省・PMDAなどとの会議・相談にアテンドした。2018年より前述のアサシス社CEOギル・

Narrative 37

# The Founder of Athersys, Inc.

## (an U.S. Ohio State bio venture), CEO (Gil), CSO (John), COO (BJ-), and SVP (Manal)

*Manal Morsy MD,PhD*

*Ivor Macleod,MBA,CPA*

*Greg PPMaufacturing Representative,SVP*

My first encounter of founder and CEO Gil Van Bokkelen, coincides with a function at the United States Embassy in Japan celebrating the U.S. Independence Day of July 4, 2017 hosted by Caroline Bouvier Kennedy, who was ending her tenure as Ambassador to Japan. I had received an email the day before from an old acquaintance, Mr. Ulrich Taglieber (U.S. Merck, VP) relaying to me that he intended to give me phone call from America, at Tokyo time 21:00 (9PM), thus requesting me to be in my office at the University of Tokyo. I was surprised to learn that after resigning from his post at Merck, Ulrich was an advisor for Athersys, Inc. After returning my office from Ambassador Kennedy's outgoing party, sure enough, at exactly 9PM his call came through in I received self-introductions by 7-8 individuals of Athersys, Inc., from which came 13 questions as well. As I responded clearly, as well as providing specific examples to heighten their understanding. Then, this tele-conference became an event to be held every week on Tuesday. An email providing the agenda of the meeting, would be sent on the previous day by Manal Morsy, (a vaccine specialist, formerly of Merck) became routine. Eventually, the phone calls were recognized as costly, thus the question/answer sessions were conducted via email. Since I became an advisor to Atersys, Inc. and from 2018 became the afore mentioned Athersys, Inc. CEO Gil Van Bokkelen's Exclusive Senior Strategic Advisor, which continues to this day.

At the time of the first tele-conference (July 4, 2017), I later learned that Gil, not mentioning his name, kept quiet and just listened. It was a rather unusual encounter. Before we

ヴァン・ボッケレンの専属（Exclusive）上級戦略アドバイザー（Senior Strategic Advisor）となり、今日に至っている。

最初の電話会議の時（2017年7月4日）、ギルは、後で知ったのだが、名乗らずに黙って聞いていた。不思議な出会いだった。いつの間にか、日本の火曜日／米国月曜日夕方に「差し」で話すようになり、今日まで続いている。今日は火曜日で、先ほど話したばかりである。家族は妻、息子と女の子（2人）の5人家族である。子煩悩な家族思いの夫でもあるし、夫婦仲は睦ましい。

ギルは、筆者と同じで酒もタバコもやらない。正直で品格（Decent）のある紳士である。アサシス社では、厳しいガバナンス（Governance）で有名だが、従業員一人一人に耳を傾け意見を聞くやさしい男でもある。特に、スタンフォード大出身のギル・ジョン・BJ－・ペリ（退職）のスタンフォード・チームの連携は見事である。ジョンの「ぶれないリーダーシップ」やBJ－の「聞く耳」、そしてマナルの百戦錬磨の経験もギルを支えている。

さて、このチームが発見開発を進めているのが、幹細胞（Stem Cell）の「マルチステム／MultiStem®」。生い立ちは、自家生（Autolougus）でなく、他家生（Allogeneic）である。臨床治験は、北海道大学病院長の寶金先生が責任者になり、全国約40施設の脳神経外科・神経内科の専門医・パラメディカルが無作為ダブルブラインド220例（TREASURE試験）の登録を本年中（2020年）の完成を目指して努力中である。そして統計的に差が出れば、先駆けも通っているので、2021年前半での承認もあり得るのである。おめでたい話である。

また、アサシス社役員会議では、ロシュ本社の研究本部長だったリー・バビス（Lee Babiss）、BBC Newsの初代編集長であったジェッフ・ランダル（Jeff Randal）、ジャーナリストのジャック・ワイゾミエルスキー（Jack Wyzomierski）によく声をかけてもらったり、意見を求められたりするのが楽しい。特に、ジェッフは自分の隣の席を空けて、「ここに座れよ」と言ってくれる。いい人だ。

knew it, we would have one-to-one conversations, every Tuesdays Japan/Monday evenings U.S. which are still ongoing today. Today is Tuesday, and I just finished speaking to him. His family of 5, includes his wife and three children, a son and two daughters. He comes across as a man who cherishes his children and a good husband, they are a typical equal-based couple.

Gil, like myself, does not drink or smoke. A gentleman who is honest and decent. Although Athersys, Inc., his strict governance is well known, he is also known as a considerate man, lending his ear to the opinions of each and every employee. Particularly, the coordination of the Stanford Team; Stanford graduates Gil, John, BJ-, and Perry (resigned) was amazing. John's [unshakable leadership], BJ- [the good listener], and Manal's [battle-hardened experience] all supporting Gil.

Well, this team is progressing the discovery and development of a stem cell [MultiStem®]. Its characteristic is that it is allogeneic, not autologous. In Japan, Healios K.K. is licensed for the rights to develop and commercialize for domestic use in treating cerebral cortex strokes. Professor Houkin of Hokkaido University is responsible for overseeing the clinical trials, involving neurosurgical, neurology specialists and paramedical, of roughly 40 medical institutions nationwide, who are placing efforts to, within the year, conduct random double-brand 220 cases (Treasuries clinical trials) to be completed within this year (2020). When the binding key opened, and statistically differences can be confirmed, and in view that it has already passed the "Saki-gake" and "Orphan designation" status, it is highly possible that it will receive approval by the early part of 2021. For Gil the first approval of [MultiStem®] will be in Japan.

## 第38話

初出：2020年8月24日

# 水・墨・金粉の水墨画家・小説家
# ——東野光生画伯

東野光生画伯

東野画伯(画伯)との出会いも、運命的であった。これを必然と言う、筆者は。昨年(2019年)9月6日(木曜日)、トルコ航空のビジネスクラスで隣り合わせだった。いつものように出発前から食事が出るまで寝ようとパーテーションを下ろしたところ、隣の「和服」の白髪の紳士が「折角ですから、お話ししませんか」と言う。「どこに何しに行くのですか…」「しかじか…これこれで」と申しますと、「私は、イスタンブール(Istanbul)の駐日トルコ大使主催の「日本文化祭り」で自分の作品について講演を頼まれ行くところです」と言う。そこで初めて、日本画家の大家と分かった次第である。イスタンブール空港に到着。通関の前で先ほどの画伯が待っていてくれ、画伯を出迎えの駐トルコ日本大使館の方が先生を連れて迎賓ゲートから通関。通関した私を待っていてくれ、日本で私のオフィスに訪ねたいとおっしゃる。

そして、10月11日突然画伯より電話。東京まで来たので、訪ねたいとのこと。この辺が並の人とは違う、画伯は。予告無しだ。赤門まで来ていただき、迎えに行きオフィスにお連れして、濃いコーヒーでお喋りをした。頃合いを見て構内のレストラン・カメリヤに案内し、ノン・アルで私の好きなメニューで食事していただいた。私のヒストリーを楽しく聞いてくれ、この次は画伯の家に招待したいと言われ帰られた。翌

Narrative 38

# Water/Ink/Gold Dust the Water & Ink Artist and Author – Master Teruo Touno

My meeting with Master Touno felt that it was destined. I would say it was inevitable. Last year, (2019) Thursday, September 6th we were seated next to each other in the business class section of Turkish Airlines. As I was preparing to bring down the window patrician, to sleep prior to take-off, until the first meal is served, as I usually do, the white-haired gentleman seated next to me said [Why not take this opportunity and talk.] [Where are you going, and what do you intend to do?], as I gave an explanation of my destination and intentions, he revealed; [I am going to Istanbul to deliver a talk on my artwork as part of a Japanese Cultural Festival sponsored by the Japanese Embassy to Turkey.] This is when I first realized that he was a master of Japanese art. Arrived at Istanbul airport. In front of customs the art master was waiting for me, he was met and taken through the VIP gate by Japanese Embassy staff. He awaited me to complete my customs processing, mentioning that he would like to visit my office in Japan.

Then, on October 11th, a sudden phone call from the art master. Taking the opportunity of traveling to Tokyo, he would like to make a visit. This is where the art master differs from ordinary people. No forewarning. He came to the Akamon (main campus gate) where upon meeting and guiding him to my office, where we enjoyed strong coffee and conversation.

When the timing was right, I guided him to the on-campus restaurant, Camelia, we enjoyed a non-alcohol meal of my preference. He happily listened to my history, and when upon departing, he invited me to visit his residence. The following year, 2020 January 16th, I received the invitation, which designated meeting at the ticket entrance of Tsushima station of

2020年1月16日早速のお招きがあり、某駅の改札で夕方6時待っているとの事。到着すると、甚平を着た画伯が待っているではないか。「よく来てくれました」と。画伯の運転する車で約15分。山里の料亭かと思うほどのたたずまい、お住まい方のお人柄がしのばれる風情でした。

すでに奥様がお出迎えで、家に上がりますと、広く長い厨房あり。お二人で料理したお頭付きの和食、続いて霜降りのビーフ・ステーキと温野菜。美味しくて、欠食児童よろしく、いい気になって食べていると、今度は収集品を見せてくれるという。これが、国宝級。拝ませてもらって…。それから、挽き立てのコーヒーをいただき、お似合いのご夫婦に馴れそめをたずねると、幼稚園、小・中学校そして大学とご一緒とか。大学で知り合うまで、それ以前のことは知らなかったと、笑い合ったという。仲睦しご夫妻である。

奥様は、本名の神藤雅子(結婚されて山本雅子)でご活躍のナーデルマン・ハープの世界の第一人者である。昨年(2019年)は、6カ月パリに滞在して、毎日(土・日無し)ナーデルマン・ハープの特訓を受けたという。CDソロ・アルバム「よみがえるナーデルマン・ハープ」をいただき、聞いてみると「何とも言えない軽やかでシャープな響きの音色で、聞きほれてしまう」、そんな感じの音色である。奥様は、日赤医療センターの音楽セラピストとして活躍中である。

画伯は小説家でもある。『浅黄の帽子』を江藤淳に見せ、「文藝」に掲載される。長編小説「似顔絵」で芸術選奨文部科学大臣新人賞を受賞。また画伯は、フロリダ州立大学の客員教授もなさっていた。とにかくスケールの大きなお人です。

私に、水墨画を描いてくれるという。本稿が当欄に掲載される頃には、画伯の水墨画が届くのではと、わくわくしている。

the Toyoko line, at 6 o'clock in the evening. Upon arriving, I found the art master, attired in a jinbei, was waiting for me. Saying, [It was good of you for coming.] A car driven by the art master took approximately 15 minutes. What appeared to be an exclusive mountain village Japanese restaurant, turns out to be his home, a residence reflecting the taste of the owner.

His wife was already outside awaiting our arrival, upon entering, there was a spacious and long kitchen. The Japanese meal that was prepared by the two of them was of fish, marbled beef steak and steamed vegetables. It was so delicious that I ate the meal with a gusto that would rival that of an undernourished child. He then offered to show me his collection, which were in the class of national treasures. I was enthralled and privileged of the opportunity. After over freshly ground coffee, I inquired on how this ideal couple met, it turns out that they attended the same kindergarten, elementary school, junior high school and university. While laughing, the couple revealed that it was not until they met at university that they were totally unaware of the past. A happily married couple.

His wife a world renown Naderman harpist who performs as Masako Endo, in her maiden name, (married name Masako Yamamoto). Studied under the late R.S. Stein (a former principal professor of harp at the Royal Academy of Music). Last year, (2019) she resided in Paris for 6 months where for everyday (except on Saturday and Sunday), she received special training of Naderman harp. I was given a CD of her solo album [A Revival of Naderman Harp], upon listening to this, [the melody was fluid punctuated with sharp timbre that is beyond words, I thoroughly enjoyed the music].

As aforementioned, the art master is also a novelist. Showing his novel, 'The Light Yellow Hat' to Jun Endo, it was published in the [Bungei]. His long novel, [Portrait] was awarded the Minister of Education, Culture, Sports and Technology New Face Award (Art Award). In addition, the art master is also a visiting professor at the Florida State University. The art master is a truly dynamic individual.

The art master has offered to paint a water & ink piece. This is a true honor, and when the piece arrives, I plan to have it published on the 40th International Pharmaceutical Magazine.

## 第39話

初出：2020年11月24日

# 米国研究製薬工業協会(PhRMA、W-DC)、日米テクニカル・コミッティー（JTC)

1986 at PhRMA in W-DC　米国研究製薬工業協会

2006年の6月頃だったと思うが、ワシントン-DCの米国研究製薬工業協会の事務所で、US-対日技術委員(Japan Technical Committee / JTC)の発足の会が開かれた。当時、筆者はE. リリーに居たが、出席した。多彩な顔触れで、メルク社の国際エクゼクテブVPであったウーリック・タグリーバー(Urick Taglieber)が議長となり、副議長をE. リリー社のボブ・ファイク(Robert Fike)が務めた。商務省デレクターのハリソン・クック(Harrison Cook)もオブザバーとして参加している。ハリソンは、今年(2020年)6月に心筋梗塞で急逝。日米双方の関係者の誰からも慕われ、惜しまれた人財であった。享年50歳、日本の大学院を出で流暢な日本語を話し、合気道を愛し、日本人の妻を愛し、一人息子ヒロキ(広樹)が居る。もう大学院であろう。ハリソンのご冥福とご家族の幸せを祈っ

Narrative 39

# The Pharmaceutical Research and Manufacturers Association (PhRMA, W-DC), US-Japan Technical Committee (JTC)

岸 圭介氏、市川俊次氏、金田 宣氏

It was around June 2006,that the inaugural meeting of the US-Japan Technical Committee (JTC) was held at the Washington, D.C. offices of the Pharmaceutical Research and Manufacturers Association. At the time, although being employed by E. Lilly, I participated in this meeting. There was a notable variety of participants, and chairing the meeting was Merck's international executive VP, Urick Taglieber, and E. Lilly's Robert Fike fulfilled the duty of vice-chair. The Director of the Department of Commerce, Harrison Cook was present in the capacity of observer. On October of 2019, Harrison suddenly passed away due to a cardiac infarction. Respected by related individuals in both Japan and the United States, his passing at the age of 50 was a great loss. Completing studies at a Japanese graduate school, he spoke fluent Japanese, with a passion for the Japanese martial art of Aikido, and a love for his Japanese wife, and his only son Hiroki, who is most likely attending graduate school. I continue to pray for the repose of Harrison's soul and his family's happiness. As for myself, Sidney Taurel, CEO of E. Lilly and the Representative of PhRMA had a discussion which lead to an amiable transfer

て止まない。私はというと、E.リリーのCEO シドニー・トウレル（Sydney Taurel）とPhRMAの代表が話し合い、円満にPhRMA に移籍、PhRMA 東京事務所（虎ノ門）で、日米欧の産官学の橋渡しを務め多忙を極める生活になった。子供の教育は、家内任せ……。

日本でも、市川さん（メルク）、岸さん（アムジェン）、庄司さん（ワイス）、金田さん（E.リリー）などの協力を得て、ジャパン・テクニカル・コミッティーを、約20社近い米国研究製薬工業協会（PhRMA）のメンバー会社と立ち上げ「ジャパン－JTC」と名付け、米国JTCと渡り合った。筆者が議長となり市川さんが書記を務めてくれ、月一の開催。市川さん、岸さん、金田さん、庄司さんと小生で世話人会を作り、議事録の確認と英訳を作り、米国PhRMAに送って一月（ひとつき）が終わる。その間、米国PhRMA会社のエクゼクティブが来日すると、厚生省（現厚労省）、アカデミアに案内し、筆者の人脈は内外共に飛躍的に拡大し、今に続いている。また若い頃、野球と陸上に明けくれた体力が今も役に立っているようである。

日米テック・コムの交流も盛んで、春秋2回2007年からほぼ十数年日米交換の来日があった。が、筆者が東大の校友会顧問・薬友会会長になりPhRMAを去り、ウーリックもメルクを定年で退職し、米国PhRMAのR&D責任者であったデービド・ウエードン（David Weadon）も米国糖尿病協会のディレクターとなり去って行き、筆者のPhRMAとの交誼は、2012年12月31日で終わった。この時多忙の中、引っ越しを手伝ってくれたのは、親友の龍雲であった。何度かトルコのイスタンブールには、元会長であった筆者とアジア医薬化学連合のシンポジウムに付き合ってくれた。

またウーリックが米国JTCを連れて来日すると、厚生省（現厚労省）、PMDA、理化学研究所、当時の内閣参与の本庶先生（2019年ノーベル医学賞）を訪ねたり、今話題の和泉内閣総理大臣特別補佐官をたずねたり、水先案内人を楽しんだ。馴れたものであった……。

ウーリック提供の前頁の写真を見れば、各社からの多彩な顔触れが見

to PhRMA, where at the Tokyo PhRMA office (Toranomon, Minato-ku, Tokyo) I started to lead an extremely busy lifestyle bridging the industry-government-academia of the U.S., Europe and Japan. I left raising the children to my wife.

In Japan, with the cooperation of Ichikawa-san (Merck), Kishi-san (Amgen), Shoji-san (Wyeth) and Kaneda-san (E. Lilly), enabled the establishment of the Japan Technical Committee, which involves close to 20 Pharmaceutical Research and Manufacturers Association (PhRMA) member companies, naming the committee as [Japan JTC], sparring with the U.S. JTC. I became the Chairman and Ichikawa-san was Secretary, a committee meeting was held once a month. Ichikawa-san, Kishi-san, Kaneda-san, Shoji-san and myself formed an Organizer Society, which was responsible for compiling and confirming the meeting minutes, translating this into English and sending this to U.S. PhRMA, would be the end of each month. In the meantime, in the event an executive of a U.S. PhRMA member corporation was to visit Japan, I would arrange visits to the Ministry of Health (currently the MHLW), interactions with the academia, rapidly developing a wide network of connections, both domestically and abroad, which continues to this day. The physical stamina that I had built during my youth, when all I did was play baseball and compete in track/field sport, paid off during these times.

The interaction between the U.S.-Japan Technical Committees were vigorous, with meetings were held twice a year in the spring and autumn from 2007 continuing over a decade, with exchanges were made between the U.S. Japan with visits to Japan. However, after I left PhRMA and becoming the Advisor of the Tokyo University Alumni Association, and Chairman of Yakuyukai, and with Urick retiring from Merck, David Weadon who was responsible for U.S. PhRMA's R&D left PhRMA to become the Director of the American Diabetes Association, my relationship with PhRMA ended on December 31, 2012. Although it was a particularly

2010 in Tokyo

える。ハリソンの顔も見える(中央当たり)。筆者も若かったです。そして、星霜幾年、私は妻を失って10年余になる。妻は小生の「わがまま」をすべて受け入れてくれ、子供の教育もすべて彼女任せ。息子は小児科医になり、娘は嫁いで(夫:大嶋尚史/半導体)大嶋姓となった。妻には、感謝をしている。孫は内・外5人となった。また、米国研究製薬工業協会の対日技術委員会の発足会議(1985年ころ)の写真は、懐かしい。最近、日本の対米技術委員会のOld Boysが集まり写真を撮った。これも懐かしい顔ぶれである。岸さん、市川さん、金田さんである。

busy period of the year, my good friend Ryu-un (Shoji-san) helped me in my relocation. He often accompanied me to symposiums, held in Istanbul, Turkey, of the Asian Federation for Medical Chemistry, of which I was a former Chairman.

When Urick would arrive in Japan with the U.S. JTC, visits were made to the Ministry of Health (the current MHLW), PMDA, the Institute of Physical and Chemical Research, as well as, to Professor Tasuku Honjyo (2019 Nobel Laureate for Medicine) who was at the time the Special Advisor to the Cabinet, and the currently talked about, Mr. Izumi, Special Assistant to the Prime Minister, I enjoyed my task as the pilot of the channels. I was really getting good at it.

The 10years-more has passed since I lost my wife (Jun) sadly. Accepting my selfishness'selflove thoughtfully, I am so grateful to Jun. Our grandchildren are now 5 ! And the photo of the first meeting of the Old Boys in Japan around Fall in 2020 is so reminiscent too ! They are Ichikawa san, Kaneda san and Kishi san.

第40話　　初出：2019年5月3日

# 2019年オーストラリア国爵位を贈られた我が師
## ——アルマレゴ博士（Dr. W. L. F. Armarego）

キャンベラ素心会
*Canberra Soshin club*

アルマレゴ博士は、私のオーストラリア国立大学（ANU）の大学院（John Curtin School of Medical Research／JCSMR）時代（1967年～1970年）のわが師（Mentor）である。「インディペンデント・シンカー（Independent Thinker／物真似はするな！）たれ、ノーベル賞を狙うような研究をしろよ」とティー・タイムで力説してくれた我が師である。偉ぶることのない人柄で、Wilfと呼んでくれというので、本稿でもWilfと呼びたい。

Wilfは英国人の両親の長男として1931年エジプトのアレキサンドリアで生まれた。小学校では、6歳年上の中西香爾（東北大学・コロンビア大学名誉教授）と一緒だったという。後に両者とも大きな仕事をすることになる。中・高教育は、英国中・高等学校（British Boys' School）で受け、1949年ロンドン大学に入学した。実際の授業はアレキサンドリア大学（University of Alexandria）で受けた。Wilfは自然科学関連の授業に自由に出席した。広いキャンパスを走っている姿が浮かぶようだ。1953年、銀時計で卒業（A BSc Special Honours degree in Chemistry）。

Narrative 40

# Dr. W. L. F. Armarego

## —— My Mentor Who was Awarded a Title from Australia in 2019

Dr. Armarego was my mentor when I was studying at the John Curtin School of Medical Research (JCSMR) of the Australian National University (ANU) from 1967~1970. My mentor was an independent thinker, "Do not imitate others!" "Conduct research targeting the Nobel Prize." Are phrases he strongly impressed upon during tea time. A non-conceited, easy-going personality, wishing to be referred to as Wilf, thus within this text I will refer to him as he preferred; Wilf.

Wilf was born in 1931 in Alexandria, Egypt as the first-born son to English parents.

In elementary school, it is said that he studied with Kouji Nakanishi, who was 6 years older, who later became Tohoku University and Columbia University's Professor Emeritus. Later, both individuals will be part of significant achievements. After receiving junior and high school education at British Boy's School, he was accepted to London University in 1949. His actual studies were conducted at the University of Alexandria. Wilf willingly attended natural science related lectures. I can almost picture him running about the spacious campus. In 1953, he graduated with a BSc Special Honors degree in Chemistry. He immediately left

すぐエジプトを離れ英国に移動。ロンドン大学（University of London）のBedford Collegeの有名な立体化学者E.E.ターナー教授（Professor E.E.Turner）の下で研究。2年で博士号（Ph.D.）を取得した。1956年、メルボルン大学有機化学の講師（A Senior Demonstrator）になり、1958年、Wilfはいよいよ ANUのJCSMRに奉職する。コーンフォース教授（Sir John Warcup "Kappa" Cornforth、1975年ノーベル化学賞）の下でのサバティカルから戻ったばかりの油の乗りきったところであった。私も恵まれていた。

そして、私がANUの奨学金の試験に合格し、ANUのJCSMRに移ったとき（1967年11月）が、我が師Wilfとの「ながーいご厚誼」の始まりである。この奨学金は凄いもので、家内と息子（1歳半）の航空券まで負担してくれ、奨学金はそれまでの給与の倍であった。1A＄が400円であった。

シドニー空港で一泊。翌朝、首都キャンベラ空港に迎えていただき、そのまま研究室に直行。金曜日だったので来週まで待たず、これからの研究テーマ（立体化学）を説明してくれた。私の研究の詳細は省くが、Wilfによると「Independent Thinker」をすぐに身に着けたと言ってくれた。ここでの3年間ほど楽しく研究だけに没頭し、また家族でピクニックに行ったりと…。私の博士論文は「SYNTHESIS, PROPERTIES AND STEREOCHEMISTRY OF REDUCED QUINAZOLINES TO TETRODOTOXIN」。

長女と次女が誕生し家族も5人になった。息子は幼稚園や近所の子供が皆白人なので、自分もオーストラリア人だと思って遊んでいたという。帰国の時には「今度はジャパンという国に住むのか」と思っていたという。子供は発想力が大人とは違うと感じた。

息子をかわいがってくれたのが、Wilfの実験助手だったピーター・グリーン（Peter Green、英国人）である。彼は、毎朝小生がキャンベラ・タイムズを買うと僕の研究室に来て、僕より前にそれを読む。そんな仲が続き、日本にもよく来ている。Wilfの指導もあり、ANUで統計学の修士号（M.Sc.）を取得し、オーストラリア政府で要職を務めた。

Egypt for England. He conducted research under the famous stereo chemist Professor E.E. Turner at Bedford College of the University of London. Acquiring a Ph. D in 2 years. In 1956, he became a lecturer of organic chemistry at the University of Melbourne and in 1958, Wilf comes to serve the JCSMR of ANU. Under Sir John Warcup "Kappa" Cornforth, 1975 winner of the Nobel Prize in Chemistry, just returning from his sabbatical and raring to go. I was extremely lucky.

I had passed an examination for a scholarship which had allowed me to study at JCSMR at the ANU, in November of 1967, the start of a [long and close] relationship with my mentor Wilf. This scholarship was impressive, for it also covered the cost of air travel tickets for my wife and son (then age 18 months old), and the scholarship amount was double my then salary. The conversion rate for 1 Australia dollar was at the time 400 yen.

Spending one night at Sydney airport. The following morning, he met at the capital's Canberra airport, going straight to the laboratory. Being a Friday, not waiting for the weekend, he explained the research theme of stereochemistry. Although I will leave out the details of my research, however, according to Wilf he told me that I was able to adapt the concept of being an'Independent Thinker'. During the 3 years there, I was able to happily concentrate on my research, as well as going on picnics with my family. My doctoral thesis was entitled'SYNTHESIS, PROPERTIES AND STEREOCHEMISTRY OF REDUCED QUINAZOLINES TO TETRODOTOXIN'.

With the arrival of my elder and second daughter, our family grew to 5. With his classmates at kindergarten and the neighborhood children his age being Caucasian, he said thought that he was Australian when he was playing with them. On returning to our home country, he said he believed he [This time I am going to live in a country called Japan]. I felt that children have a different way of perception than adults.

*Miss. Masako Amemiya*
東大法学部院生申請の日系
オーストラリアンの学生
雨宮正子さん

Wilf's laboratory assistant Peter Green, who was British, was fond of my son. Every morning I would buy an edition of the Canberra Times and place it on my lab table, he would come by and read the newspaper before me. This relationship continued; he also makes frequent visits to Japan. Through Wilf's guidance he obtained a M. Sc. in Statistics from ANU and currently holds an important post within the Australian government.

第41話　　初出：2020年12月14日

# 小林 喜光
## ―― 素早く勇気ある決断の出来る男

最近の小林喜光氏の決断(2020年11月23日)、三菱ケミカルHDにジョンマーク・ギルソン氏(Jean-Marc Gilson)を社長に招いたのを見ても、その鋭さがよく解る。ギルソン氏が、ベルギー出身なのも懐かしい感じがする。三菱油化時代(1970年代)、ベルギーには4半期ごとに出張し導入先のC社を訪問し製法特許の打ち合わせ、副作用の解明など。いそがしいが、楽しかった。夜は世界3大フレンチ・レストランのビラロネーヌ(Lavillaine)に招かれ、最後は葉巻で締めくくり。C社交渉役のクヌート氏(Cnute)も懐かしい。よく面倒を見てくれた。

最初に喜光氏にお会いしたのは、2000年代後半の時期である。元三菱油化の門脇修一郎氏(当時日本全薬工業取締役)のアレンジによるものであった。当時、善光氏は、デュポン(DuPont)のようになりたいと新聞に書いていた。しかし、三菱ケミカルHDはデュポンにないものを持っていた。田辺三菱製薬である。その特徴を生かすべきであると進言し、嘉光氏と会うことになった。前もって筆者の『国際人になるためのInsight Track』を謹呈した。2008年くらいだった気がする。三菱ケミ

## Narrative 41

# Yoshimitsu Kobayashi

## —— A Man Who Was Capable of Making Quick and Courageous Decisions

The recent decision (October 23, 2020) made by Mr. Yoshimitsu Kobayashi was to invite Mr. Jean-Marc Gilson as president of Mitsubishi Chemical HD, where he is chairman, reflecting his acuteness. Mr. Gilson who is from Belgium, gave me a sense of nostalgia. When I was with Mitsubishi Petrochemical Co., Ltd. (1970's), every quarter I would go on a business trip to Belgium to have meetings on matters such as; a manufacturing process patent and clarifying side effects, with C company, a firm which was introducing a product. Although hectic, it was enjoyable. Evenings, I would be invited to dine at one of the world's 3 most celebrated French restaurant Lavillaine, where after the meal would be offered a cigar. C company's negotiator was Mr. Cnute, who also conjures nostalgic memories. He really looked after me.

The first time I met Mr. Yoshimitsu was in 2008. The meeting was arranged by Mr. Shuichiro Kadowaki, formerly of Mitsubishi Chemical (at the time he a director at Nippon Zenyaku Kogyo Co., Ltd.) It was a time when Mr. Yoshimitsu had written how he aspired to become like Dupont in a newspaper. However, Mitsubishi Chemical HK possessed something that Dupont did not, which is Tanabe Mitsubishi Pharma. The reason I met with Mr. Yoshimitsu was to directly advise him of this specific feature. Prior to the meeting I presented him with my publication [Insight Track – To Become an International Minded Person]. We met at the head quarter offices of Mitsubishi Chemical HD which are located in the Marunouchi area. I had written on a sheet of A4 size paper [The Necessity of Re-Examining the Pharmaceutical Business] and handed this to Mr. Yoshimitsu. The manager of the office of the president accepted this, and later the project was established. I heard that the president of Tanabe Mitsubishi Pharmaceuticals, Mr. Mitsuka, was originally from Tanabe Pharmaceuticals, and with the change to the current president, Mr. Ueno, the firm came under the leadership of Mitsubishi. In addition, their pharmaceutical business was to be into absorbed into Mitsubishi Chemical. When considering aspects of managing information and intellectual property, it was a wise strategy.

Now, to speak about Mr. Yoshimitsu, after concluding his master's studies at the School of Science of the University of Tokyo, he went on scholarly battles; studying physics at the

カルHDの本社(丸の内)でお会いした。A4紙一枚に「医薬事業の見直しの必要性」を喜光氏に手渡した。社長室長が受け取り、後にプロジェクトが出来た、と聞いている。田辺三菱製薬社長も田辺製薬出身から、三津家氏そして現社長の上野氏に代わり三菱主導になった。更に今回、その医薬事業を三菱ケミカルに取り込んだという。情報管理、知的財産の管理を考えると、喜光氏の賢明な戦略である。

さて、喜光氏の語るに、東大理学部の博士課程(Ph.D.を取得)を修了し、イスラエル(Israel )の テル–アビブ大学(Tel Avir University)・イルサレム大学( Jerusalem University)と転戦し、ここでもPh.D.取得している。イスラエルに行くとき、見合いをして互いに一目ぼれ! 結婚したのが、現夫人である。帰国して三菱化成の面接で、赤ズボンに緑のポロシヤツ姿。採用した社長(筆者の友人)も偉かった。後は、トントン拍子の出世街道。

もう一つ忘れない喜光氏との交遊は、大相撲である。筆者の茨城県立水海道高校の同級生で、器械のリース会社で成功した草間春正氏が、二段目の桟敷(4人)を持っており、経済同友会代表幹事になっていた喜光氏夫妻を招いて相撲観戦した。はじめは、狭くてぎこちなくても、ものの30分も過ぎると、4人がうまく収まるものである。熱狂的に稀勢の里を応援した。が、喜光氏は豪栄道がひいきのようであった。顔がいいと言っていた。愉快なことに、日本の将来とか日米医薬産業とかの話に夢中で、これより三役になって「少し相撲を見ようよと云うありさまで……」。こんなことが、数年続き3人がお互いのいい所を理解し良い友人になった。最近、ホテルのトイレでばったり。イヨウ! といった具合である。とにかく同友会代表幹事として、三菱ケミカルHD会長として「歯に衣着せぬ」論客ぶりは、有名である。ガバナンスの欠如に苦しんだ東芝の社外取締役としても、妥協を許さない辣腕ぶりは有名だった。三菱ケミカルHDはガバナンス先進企業としても有名であるが、今度は、株式会社日本(ジャパン・インク)のガバナンスを主導してもらいたい。米国大統領との経済戦略に期待したいものである。

Hebrew University of Jerusalem, and chemistry at the University of Pisa in Italy. This was followed by his attaining a Ph. D. in Science from the University of Tokyo. When he was going to Israel, he attended an arranged meeting with a potential spouse, where they both fell in love at w sight! Resulting in the marriage with his current wife. Upon returning to Japan, he went to his job interview with Mitsubishi Kasei Co., Ltd. wearing red trousers and a cotton polo shirt. Praise should be given to the president (my friend) who hired him. What followed was an unhindered path to promotions.

Another unforgettable companionship with Mr. Yoshimitsu is Sumo wrestling. My friend, Mr. Masaharu Kusama, who was in the same grade at Tochigi Prefectural Mitsu Kaido High School, and is currently a successful owner of a machine leasing firm, possesses for the second time an exclusive seating area for 4 individuals, invited Mr. Yoshimitsu, who had become the Chairman of the Keizai Doyukai, and his wife to view a Sumo tournament. He was wildly cheering for the Grand Champion Kise no Sato. However, it seems that Mr. Yoshimitsu favors Go Ei Doh. He noted that he had a good face. What is enjoyable is while passionately talking about the future of Japan and the U.S. Japan pharmaceutical industry, when it comes to the matches involving the three highest ranks, [it comes to "Let's watch some Sumo."] Over several years, situations such as this have led to the three of us to establish an understanding of each other's positive aspects, and becoming good friends.

Recently, I unexpectedly ran into him at the restroom of a hotel. Hi! Was the familiar greeting. As Chairman of the Doyukai, Chairman of Mitsubishi Chemical HD, he is famous for his forthright manner in expressing his thoughts. This was strongly evident during his tenure as an outside director for Toshiba, which was struggling with issues surrounding the absence of corporate governance, he was noted for not permitting any compromise with great shrewdness. Although Mitsubishi Chemical HD is known for being a leading corporation in corporate governance, next time it would be ideal to have him lead the governance of K.K. Japan, Japan Inc. Expectations rise toward a meeting on economic strategies with the U.S. President.

第42話　　初出：2019年12月9日

# 小宮山 宏（第28代東京大学総長）現在、株式会社三菱総合研究所理事長 ―― 先駆者となる勇気

東京大学が法人化した当時の東大総長としての言葉“先頭に立つ勇気”には感銘を受けた。先生は、総長時代には大学法人化による組織改革と教育・研究改革を実施されたが、“プラチナ社会”の主宰者であることでもよく知られている。私が解説するまでもないが、先生は、自宅を開放して（NHK TV）、自ら省エネの効果をデータを示して説明をする。理論派であると同時に実践家でもある。地球の資源の有限性に着目してまとめた「成長の限界」で有名なローマ・クラブの会員である。

先生は、とにかく明るい。奥様もそうだ。似た者夫婦である。先生には大相撲などでよく呼び止められる。私も外資系が長くオハイオ州クリーヴランドやワシントンDCにオフィスがある。先生は､西のハーバード（Harvard）と言われるスタンフォード（Stanford）と縁が深い。奥様も、ご子息も、お嬢さんも東大卒。弟君（小宮山眞：私とウマが合う）も東大卒。まあ～、いわば東大一家と言ったところである。

先生は、言わずと知れた“プラチナ社会”の主宰者である。プラチナ社会については世間にもよく理解されており、私が語るに落ちることもないと思う。2004年、東大総長の時、“知の構造化”を発表している。人

Narrative 42

# Hiroshi Komiyama (28th President of the University of Tokyo) Currently Chairman of the Mitsubishi Research Institute, Inc.

## —— The Courage of Being a Forerunner

As president of the University of Tokyo, when it was incorporated, I was impressed by his words "the courage of being a forerunner". Dr. Komiyama, during his tenure as president of the University of Tokyo is known for conducting organizational, education and research reform through the incorporation of the institution, becoming the president of this 'platinum' corporation. It is not for me to go into the details, for Dr. Komiyama disclosing his residence, for a program broadcasted by NHK TV, in which he explains in detail, while providing his own data on the effects of energy conservation. A theorist, at the same time, a man of practice. Focusing on the limitation of the earth's resources, he compiled [Growth's Limitation], and he is a member of the famous World Knowledge Dialogue Scientific Board.

Dr. Komiyama is an undeniably cheerful individual. As is his wife. They are a couple who share similarities. He is frequently called to a stop when he visits Sumo tournaments. I also have a long relationship with foreign capital corporations, and have offices in Cleveland, Ohio and Washington D.C. Dr. Komiyama has a strong relationship with Stanford, which is referred to as the Harvard of the west. His wife, son and daughter are all University of Tokyo graduates. His younger brother, Makoto Komiyama (who I get along well) is also a graduate. Well, they can be referred to as a University of Tokyo family.

Dr. Komiyama is the president of the undoubtable 'platinum corporation'. As what the term 'platinum corporation' represents is understood by the public, I do not believe that is necessary for me to go into a narrative. In 2004, as president of the University of Tokyo, he announced the 'Structuration of Knowledge'. This refers to a structure in which the vast knowledge possessed by the human race would be effectively utilized. As aforementioned, it is precisely this that connects to his opening his own energy effective residence. Recently, he talks about a sustainable corporation. These days, I have found that many individuals frequently write the English word; sustainability. It seems to be a reflection of the perception that if you are satisfied with what you have today, you would like to sustain this, well, for the time being.

類の持つ知識は膨大となったが、それを有効活用して実践するのが、構造化であるという。まさに前述のご自宅のエコハウスの公開がそのものである。最近、持続可能性社会（Sustainability）を語っている。最近よくSustainabilityという英語を書いている個人を見かける。どうも、今の日常に満足していれば、持続させたい——ある時まで。そんな感じを受ける。畏れながら自分も現在に満足なので。しかし、小宮山氏は、社会に目を向けて持続可能性を見ている。素晴らしいことである。日本ほど、福利厚生に秀でた国は世界にない。しかし、2050年位になると世界人口の50％がアフリカ地域に生存すると言われている。そこでは、いかにして少子化を進めるかが焦点になり、先進国家とは真逆になる。先生のお知恵に頼りたい。

前述の“先頭に立つ勇気”は、東大は最高学府と言われる（事実そうである）一方、世間は厳しく、メディアはよくネガティブな面を取り上げる。この時に、この言葉はあることを気付かせてくれた。堂々と名乗れば、いいじゃないかと。私は、東大校友会顧問と東大薬友会会長をしている。これを絆として世間との交流を深め、世のため、他人（ヒト）のために尽くすことである。最近、よく人に助けられうれしいことが増えている。ありがたいことです。情けは他人（ヒト）のためならずである。

また、ある構内パーティーの席で、私がノーベル賞について「待っていては取れない、取りに行くものである」と話したときに、「そう…」と言ったのをよく覚えている。それは、2005年にノーベル物理学賞を受賞した米国国立標準技術研究所（NIST）のジョン・ホール（John Hall）、オーストラリアの30数年来の親友ピーター・アンドリュース（Peter Andrews：Johnの友人、現在クイーンズランド州政府科学アドバイザー）と私の3人で京都の祇園で食事をした時にジョンが言うには、ジョンの同賞同時受賞者のドイツのマックス・プランク研究所長であるハンシュ氏（Theodor W. Hansch）が“ノーベル賞を取りたいのなら、米国人でイスラエル系の人と組むのがいいんだ”と言ったという。小生には、それがヒッカカッテいて、そんな話を先生に言った時だったのである。

This is what can be felt. A satisfaction of an individual with their own current existence with a sense of fear. However, Mr. Komiyama is looking at sustainability through placing attention toward society. It is a truly wonderful approach. There is no other country as Japan, that has established a superior welfare system. Yet, by the year 2050, it is said that 50% of the global population will be located in the African region. It is there that focus is on advancing birth control, a total reverse of developed nations. We will need to borrow Dr. Komiyama's knowledge.

As aforementioned "the courage of being a forerunner", stems from when the University of Tokyo was referred to as the highest institution of education (which it actually is), on the other hand, the public was severe, and there was a tendency within the media to report negatively. It was during this period, that I realize is why these words exist. There is nothing wrong in announcing one's self with confidence. I myself, am an advisor to the University of Tokyo Alumni Association, and chairman of the University of Tokyo Pharmaceutical Sciences Society. It is through these bonds that I deepen my interactions with society, and devote myself to the overall wellbeing of society, and people. Recently, I am the happy recipient of an increasing amount of assistance from others. For this, I am grateful. Mercy is not an emotion toward another, but in fact is an emotion that benefits oneself.

In addition, on the occasion of an on-campus party, referring to the Nobel Prize, I mentioned [It cannot be won by waiting, going after it is the way to win it], I vividly remember that he said [Yes...] This goes back to 2005 when John Hall of the National Institute of Standards and Technology, won the Nobel Prize in Physics, and a close friend of over 30 years of Australia, Peter Andrews, who is a friend of John, who is currently a scientific advisor to the government of Queensland and myself had dinner within Kyoto's Gion district. According to John, the Max Planck Institute director, Theodor W. Hansch, who won the same Nobel Prize at the same time as John, said "If you want to win the Nobel Prize, it would be beneficial to team up with an American of Jewish descent". Personally, this statement had stuck to my mind, which led me to share this with Dr. Komiyama.

第43話

# 長井長義とテレーゼ夫人

長井長義とテレーゼ夫人(婚約直前の記念写真)

さて、表題の「長井長義とテレーゼ夫人」については、多くの方々がいろんな機会をとらえてお書きになっている。それらをあまり気にせずに、私なりに筆を進めていきたい。

長井長義は、秀吉の親友だった、かの有名な蜂須賀小六の土佐藩(蜂須賀大名)の藩医の家に生まれた(1845年)。

明治政府誕生3年前の日本の夜明け前だ。徳川幕府の有力大名だった当時の蜂須賀大名

*Michio Ui*
宇井理生先生
エールリッヒ・コッホ賞受賞(1991)

## Narrative 43

# Professor Nagayoshi Nagai and his wife Therese Schumacher

About the famous love-story of the couple, quite a few people have been writing in many opportunities and /or circumstances. But I would refrain this time. The intention of Prof. Hoffmann was「So adapted to Germany, Nagai with Therese should be a prototype of successful international marriage IN JAPAN.

Born in 1845 as the first son of Medical Doctor served to the famous Daimyo (Federal Lord) / Koroku Hachisuka, whose first generation was a good friend of Sho-gun Hideyoshi, once upon once time, was Nagayoshi Nagai in Tosa-area (now, Ko-chi Prefecture). Due to the good friendship with Sho-gun Hideyoshi, the Hachisuka Daimyo had been respected and well-accepted among other Daimyos well and in public as well. Through Hachisuka's leadership, Hachisuka-Daimyo was successful to get one young therefrom among around 10 that the Meiji Government plans to send to Europe including the UK to study therein civilization and its culture.

But, before that, the Tosa-Daimyo sent Nagayoshi to Nagasaki-City that was open to Europe only that time, in efforts to learn and be trained about overseas. When he arrived at Edo-City of Tokugawa Government, He was surprised with pleasantly! Just the three (3) years before start-up of Meiji-Government. He was involved in learning and training for three years there. Then, he left Japan in 1871 onboard to Berlin in Germany at age of 26.

When he arrived at Berlin, he visited faculty of Medicine and also looked into Faculty of Science. There, He was so much shocked with a new experience which can't be experienced in then-Medicine. That was「two different substances reacted in solvent to give rise to A NEW PRODUCT」. Then, he asked Faculty of Science to arrange a meeting with its Head, Prof. Hoffmann. When they met each other, Prof. Hoffmann was so impressed with the Japanese young in a fully self-confidence and appearance. He gave the J-young a laboratory-bench for organic synthetic chemistry.

は、幕府が西洋留学に選んだ十数名の中の一人を土佐藩から送り出すことに成功した。それが、藩医の長男・長井長義であった。土佐藩の「人材（人財）育成先見の明」がうかがえるのは、それ以前に長井青年（16歳）を長崎に内地留学させていることである。

幕府のあったお江戸に初めて到着した長井は、維新政府／明治政府の新しい文化の息吹に圧倒された。「これが、江戸か！」。ちょうど明治政府創設の3年前である。新政府の海外留学の心構えの研修と手続き経て、ドイツ医学を学ぶべく、ベルリンに向けて出港した。時に1871年、26歳。

ベルリン到着後、直ちにベルリン大学医学部に行ったが、理学部も訪ねた。当時のベルリン大学の有機化学は世界最高で、リービッヒ教授の一番弟子ホフマンが教授であった。そこで、長井は違う物体が液体の中で化学反応を起こし新しい物質が生まれるという現象を見て、驚嘆した。当時の医学では考えられないことであった。ホフマン教授に頼み込み、有機合成の実験台を借り受けた。この辺の行動力や、まさに長井自身のリーダーシップの片りんを見る思いだ。

また、テレーゼ夫人との恋愛については、多くの方が書いておられるので、今回筆者は遠慮したいと思う。ホフマン教授が意図したのは、「それほど性分があったドイツ国なのだから、ドイツ女性と結婚をして日本に住んで“日本における国際結婚の先駆者・成功者となり、その日本で仲良く生涯の伴侶として暮らせよ”」ということだったと感じている。

しかし、帰国した長井氏（1887年）に、医学部の教授席はもはや無く、理学部には元々ない。そこで、目を付けたのは、医学部薬学科である。生薬中心だった薬学に有機化学分野を導入しようとして長井氏を招き入れたのである。そして、東大薬学が日本の有機化学のメッカにもなったのである。

また、私がこの偉人の後輩として第39代薬友会会長（2010年～）に就いているのは、恐れ多いことでもある。

During stay there（3 years）, he synthesized「Ephedrin / Brancodilater」,even now over 100 years prescribed.

Great !

But, when he returned to Japan in 1887, he has no chair at Medicine, of course in Science. Rescued him was Faculty of Pharmaceutical Science. The strain of the faculty was Herb-Medicine, and wanted to start-up Organic Chemistry. The objective of the both was comparable in happiness. The Faculty has come to Mecca of organic Chemistry in Japan.

And as a junior to this great person, I am so lucky to be the Chairman of Yakuyukai（2010~）.

長井長義先生が、初代の薬友会会長で、私が第39代会長。（就任祝の写真）

Globalization
つれづれに人（ひと）を敬う

# 第4章
## 特別話

Globalization

# Respecting People As the Time is Passing

## Article 4

## Special Storty

## グローバリゼーション
## つれづれに、人(ひと)を敬う

# 日本の文化

聖徳太子 574～622(48歳の生涯)
*Shotoku Taishi*

空海（真言宗開祖） 774～835（60歳の生涯）
*Kukai*

## グローバリゼーション
## つれづれに、人(ひと)を敬う

# 日本の武道(空手と居合抜き)

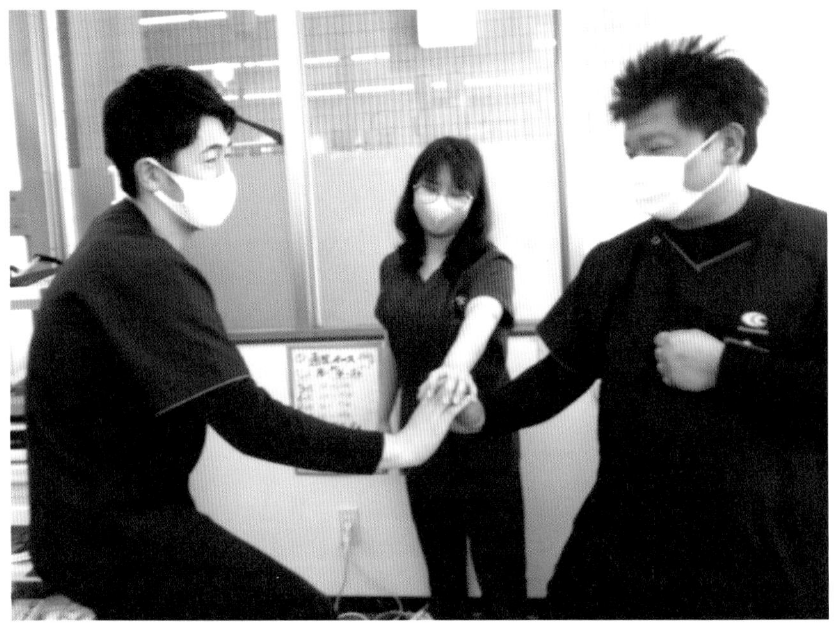

内田悠斗（忍者初段、1997～）　日吾文香（女性審判）　渡邊亮太（空手4段、1987～）

吉宮隆彦
（居合抜き6段、1943～）

特別話　　初出：2019年10月14日

# 春日通り・本郷通りの友だち

まず、ヨシミ・フォト・スタジオの布施敏夫さんだ。とにかく親切で、動きが早くてついて行けない。美人の奥さんとお嬢さんがいる。私の公式写真はすべて撮っていただいている。挙句、正面に飾ってくれるので、ありがたい。時々知らない大学人から挨拶をいただく。うれしいですね。私の構内オフィスにもよく来てくれ、片付けをしてくれる。掛値のない本当の親友である。少し戻ると、コーヒーのAmmoniteがある。布施さんとよく落ち合うところでもある。そして中華店・萬成園がある。中国人陳さんとその奥さんがともに親切で週一で食べに行く。

本郷通りにきてまず構内側を行くとスターバックスがあり、親切な後藤さんがいて、ブラックエプロンの福島君と長谷川さんがいた。彼は独立して自分の店を持ち、彼女は上野店に移った。ちょっと行くと、寛永堂本郷赤門店があり、ここの若鮎はおいしい。さらに上っていくと御殿（レストラン）がある。看板娘の加藤さんがいて店長の池内さんと副の佐藤さんがいる。ここのカレーは天下一品だが１日５食と少ない。

さて本郷通りの左側に行くと本富士警察署の交番がある。上っていくとホームショップやすのがあり、店主の安野さんがいつも座っている。ちょっとしたものは、たいてい間に合って便利である。ちょっと行くと立野画廊がある。棟方志功の本物が置いてあったりする。立野さんは、布施さんの親友であるが、ちょっと違う。日常の頼みごとはすぐにやってくれるが、長い目でこれこれを探してくれと言うと、自分が興味がな

## Special Story

# Friends of Kasuga Avenue & Hongo Avenue

Let we start with Yoshimi Photo Studio's Toshio Fuse-san. Ultimately friendly, moving so swiftly that it is difficult to keep up. He has a beautiful wife and daughter. I have always had my official portraits to be taken by him. Ultimately, displaying the photo in the entrance to his studio, I am grateful. This has brought about greetings from individuals at the University, that I do not know. A pleasant experience. Often making visits to my office on campus, where he assists in clearing and organizing. An irreplaceable true friend. Going back a little, one can find the coffee shop Ammonite. Fuse-san and I often use this place to meet up. Then there is the Chinese restaurant: Man Sei En. The establishment is run by a Chinese gentleman, Chin-san and his wife, who are both extremely friendly, where I have lunch there one a week.

Traveling on Hongo Avenue on the campus side, there is a Starbucks, where the friendly Goto-san is present along with Fukushima-kun and Hasegawa-san both wearing their black aprons. He has become independent and has opened his own establishment, she has transferred to the shop in Ueno. A short distance takes one to Kan Ei Doh Hongo Akamon Branch, their Japanese confectionary know as 'Waka Ayu' is delicious. A further climb and you can find the restaurant 'Goten'. The draw girl, Kato-san is there along with manager, Ikeuchi-san and co-manager, Sato-san. The curry they serve is the best ever, but unfortunately only a limited 5 servings are made per day.

Now traveling on the left side of Hongo Avenue a Kohban (police box) of the Moto Fuji Police Department can be found as the guardian of the area. Climbing the avenue, there is the home shop 'Yasuno' can be found, the owner Yasuno-san can be seen always sitting within. A

いと動かない。

さらに上っていくとパーコーメンの瀬佐味亭がある。ここのパーコーは、実にシャキシャキとしてうまい。2度揚げしているのだろうか。そしてついにボン・アート(Bon-Art)にたどり着く。ここには、フロアマネジャーの峰岸さんがおり、渡邉カルピスさんがいて、店長の久保田さんがいる。社長の尚さんこと染谷尚人さんがいる。本郷美術骨董館を経営している。毎週火曜日は、カルピスさんが料理する(つくる)パスタを食べる。いろんなパスタを創造する(つくる)が、ベーコンペペロンチーノがいいかな。峰岸さんは、わたくしの本『国際人になるためのInsight Track』と『素心』を店の書棚において宣伝してくれる。感謝である。俳優・梅宮辰夫氏の父親は満州医大を卒業後、帰国。このボン・アートの土地に落ち着き東大病院に勤務。梅宮辰夫氏が骨董店の名誉館長を務めているのも納得である。尚さんの心か。

赤門前に来ると扇屋がある。ここのカステラは、長崎は福砂屋にも負けないというのが扇屋さんの自慢。さらに行くと赤門餃子軒がある。中国湖南省からの料理人(2人)で無口だが腕はすごい。何を頼んでも、美味いと舌が言う。

ここでどうしても触れたい人が居る。少し離れるが、英国大使館の北側のカットサロンタカハシ(髪切り／Haircutter)である。店長の高橋さんの腰回りは、トビの親方よろしくハサミ、クシ、カミ・カッター・レーザーなどを腰ベルトに巻いている。最近、髪には白いものがだいぶ増えた、歳なりだね。もう一人、私にとっては世界一の腕自慢の理髪師がいる。斎藤さんだ。最後の熱いタオルは、顔に当てると温泉気分になる。英国大使館では斎藤さんで通っている。共に良き友人である。

variety of items of necessity can be found, which makes this shop convenient. Traveling a little further will bring you to Tateno Gallery. A genuine Shiko Munakata can be found. Although Tateno-san is a good friend with Fuse-san, there is a difference. An everyday request is met with immediate action, however, if it incurs a long-term view as a request to look for a particular item, if he has no interest, he will not pursue it.

Climbing further there is the establishment of 'Sesami Tei' which serves Hainan noodles. Their Hainan noodles have a wonderful texture and are delicious. Perhaps it is due to the double deep fry process. Finally, one has arrived at 'Bon Art'. It is here that floor manager Negishi-san, Kalupis Watanabe-san, and manager Kubota-san can be found. The president Nao-san, otherwise known as the 'Dyer Naoto-san is also present. He runs the 'Hongo Bijyutsu Kotto Kan' (arts and antiques). Every Tuesday, I eat the pasta that Kalupis-san cooks. Although there are various creations with pasta, I personally think the bacon pepperoncino is good. Negishi-san lines my book: 'To Become an International Individual Insight Track' on the bookshelf, advertising the publication. Of which I am grateful. The actor, Tatsuo Umemiya's father, after graduating from Manchuria Medical College, returned to Japan. He settled on the property that is now 'Bon Art' and was employed at the University of Tokyo Hospital. Thus, it makes sense that Mr. Tatsuo Umemiya was the honorary chairman of this antique shop. Perhaps it was due to Nao-san's heart.

At Akamon Mae there 'Oogi Ya'. They boast that their castella may not be defeated by that made by Nagasaki's 'Fukusaya'. Going further there is the 'Akamon Gyoza Ken'. Two chefs from China's Hunan Province are, although quiet, are extremely capable. Any dish is delicious, according to the palate.

There is an individual that I must touch upon. A distance away, on the northern side of the British Embassy is the 'Cut Salon Takahashi'. Wrapped around the hip of manager Takahashi-san, is a belt worthy of a Japanese carpenter's tool belt, lined with scissors, comb, haircutter, and razor. Recently, inevitable with my age, I have noticed an increase in white (grey) hairs. There is another barber that I would boast is perhaps the best in the world. This is Saito-san. The last steamed towel, when placed on my face, makes me feel like I am in an 'onsen' (hot spring). At the British Embassy, I go for Saito-san. They are both good friends.

## グローバリゼーション
## つれづれに、人(ひと)を敬う

# 特任秘書としてお手伝いいただいた方々に感謝

布施 敏夫 …… 善美写真

峰岸 香代子 …… ボン・アート

染谷 尚人 …… ボン・アート

久保田 直樹 …… ボン・アート

元山 和泉 …… ボン・アート

渡辺 カルピス …… ボン・アート

田中 明彦 …… 産学連携

富永 広三 …… アップジョン

加藤 千春 …… 御殿

佐藤　忍 …… 御殿

須賀 登志雄 …… 御殿

池内 遊気 …… 御殿

| | | |
|---|---|---|
| 三宅 留美 | …… | ボリショイバレエ |
| 吉田 由紀子 | …… | 薬友会事務局 |
| 後藤 玄 | …… | プリンティング・サービス |
| 篠塚 裕太 | …… | 指圧治療 |
| 村上 里緒夏 | …… | 指圧治療 |
| 中野 麗弥 | …… | 指圧治療 |
| 柏原 由明 | …… | 三菱油化 |
| 赤坂 恵里華 | …… | 三菱油化 |
| 森田 賢一 | …… | 千葉銀行 |
| 高橋 良和 | …… | 幸和商事 |
| 吉田 慶子 | …… | ハウス・クリーン |
| 佐藤 直樹 | …… | 指圧治療 |
| 池田 侑平 | …… | 指圧治療 |
| 高橋直也 | …… | 指圧治療 |

## グローバリゼーション
## つれづれに、人(ひと)を敬う

# 茨城県立水海道第一高等学校

(昭和29年度卒業生、男子225名・女子25名)

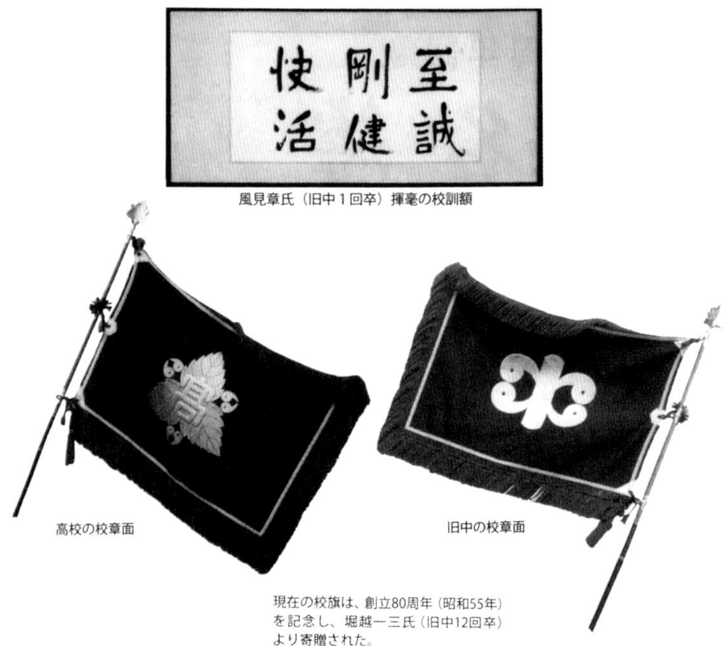


風見章氏(旧中1回卒)揮毫の校訓額

高校の校章面

旧中の校章面

現在の校旗は、創立80周年(昭和55年)を記念し、堀越一三氏(旧中12回卒)より寄贈された。

## 校歌

東京音楽学校　教授　吉丸一昌　作詞
東京音楽学校助教授　南　能衛　作曲

筑波の山は雲を衝き
鬼怒の流れは四十五里
空のあなたに舟の帆白し
ここぞわれらが祖先の地

むかし天下を睥睨の
東国男子の魂は
なほ三寸の胸にあり

振へ振へもろともに
負けじ心を振り起せ
いざやいざやわが友
負けじ心を振り起せ

旧講堂

現在の正門

# 昭和29年度卒業生(男子225名・女子25名)
# 早世の小林 利(登志)女医

「かわらじの白椿」

素心館クラブ有志
小林五左衛門　十世(利彦)宅

同級生だった彼女の仲よし
星野成子(書家)氏に深謝する。
2010年ころ

高校卒業時の写真(1958年3月)
1936 − 1960、24とせの生涯
早60年

小林医院のある守谷市で
「サロン・ド・カフェ よしだ」を営む
吉田義雄氏

# 52になった次女陽子のお祝いに

（1969年9月16日—1991年5月19日／2021年5月19日）

彼女は、1969年9月16日、オーストラリア国首都キャンベラ市オーストラリア国立大学病院にて誕生した。同じく、キャンベラ生まれの長女夏子（現姓：大嶋夏子／夫：大嶋尚史／孫：美希・宏一））と1年違い（1968年9月14日）である。共に、大英帝国国籍であった。後に、日本国籍も取得。帰国後、我孫子市東小学校・湖北台中学校を経て、東洋大学短期大学英文科を卒業。その間、高校時代にロンドンにてHomestayを、そして夏休みには、当時小生がDivision Vice Presidentとして勤務していた米国アップジョン（Upjohn and Company 、米国ミシガン州カラマズー市）に滞在し米国生活も経験している国際派で、意見をハッキリ言う物おじしない子であった。短大卒業後、地元の千葉銀行東京本社国際部の勤務となった。たまたま行った筑波市（現つくば市）にて、不慮の事故により、親友と共に1991年5月19日（日曜日）に天に召された。これは、私たち家族にとっては、生き続ける限り背負う宿命となったが、強く生きようと誓い合った。

# 「とんぼのめがね」

額賀誠志 作詞・平井康三郎 作曲

とんぼの　めがねは
水いろ　めがね
青いおそらを
とんだから　とんだから

とんぼの　めがねは
ぴか　ぴか　めがね
おてんとさまを
みてたから　みてたから

とんぼの　めがねは
赤いろ　めがね
夕焼雲(ゆうやけぐも)を
とんだから　とんだから

# エピローグ

## 著者よ、本書『敬人　つれづれに人(ひと)を敬う』を書いた意図は何だったのか

まず、『敬人　つれづれに人(ひと)を敬う』という本をどうして書けるようになったのか。どのようにして、お会いした方々(人物)と会う機会に恵まれたのか。米国アップジョン社・E. リリー社でのデヴィジョン・バイス・プレジデントを通じて、また米国研究製薬工業協会(Washington DC)の対日技術代表を通して、また東京大学校友会顧問・東京大学薬友会会長を通して 多くの尊敬すべき人物に出会う機会があり、過去の人も含めその足跡を読者の皆様にお伝えしたかったのが、この本『敬人　つれづれに人(ひと)を敬う』発刊の経緯である。例えば、アレキサンダー大王を書いた時は、今のマケドニアに一週間の一人旅をして彼の真実の現証をした。しかも、私にとってはすべて先生であるが、敬愛する先達・親友を話題の人物として選んでも、そのタイトルには本当に苦労した。最近のバッフェット氏の場合、「木から滑っても、なお男」など。選んだ人物の魅力を端的に読者の皆様にどのようにお伝えするのか、話題一つを書き上げるのに結構時間を掛けている。「国際医薬品情報」の編集長や編集女史とは、一字一句、お互い納得いくまで打ち合わせを何度も行う。そうでないと楽しく読んでいただけない。

読者のみなさまに、少しでも筆者を知っていただくため、大変僭越ですが私どもの家系にふれさせていただきたい。比較をするのは烏滸がましいが、彼の漱石先生と同じ名主の出身である。いわゆる旧家である。

第八代将軍徳川吉宗の享保の改革(1716年～1737年)の六項目の一つである重農主義のために、筑波山と利根川(坂東)の中間の沼地帯を開墾して田畑にするために送り込まれた浄土真宗の一向宗の宗徒で、平の将門を信奉して現在に至る家系である。なので、成田山新勝寺(平安朝廷

# Epilogue

Author, I wrote this article "Globalization: Respect for People"
What was the intention.

As the author, what was my intent in writing, [Globalization – Respecting People I Pass the Time], and what enabled me to write [Globalization – Respecting People I Pass the Time].

The memorable events that had allowed me the opportunities to encounter remarkable individuals who appear in this book. The American corporations of Upjohn and E. Lilly where through Vice President, as well as my experiences as the Japan Technical Representative for the Pharmaceutical Research and Manufacturers Association (Washington D.C.), as Advisor to the University of Tokyo Alumni Association, and Chairman of the University of Tokyo Yakuyukai (pharmacology alumni), may have very well contributed greatly, to, and the essence behind the publication of this book [Globalization – Respecting People I Pass the Time]. For example, when I wrote the narrative on Alexander the Great, I endeavored a trip alone to present day Macedonia in an attempt to retrace and review the actual events surrounding Alexander. Furthermore, I was faced with great difficulties in selecting an appropriate title for the narratives which described individuals whom I regarded with the utmost respect and affection, my seniors who I revere as my teachers of everything, and stories of close friends. Such as in the case of the recent narrative on Mr. Warren Buffett, [Even Slipping from a Tree, the Man]. In hopes to straightforwardly convey, to readers, the fascinating aspects of the chosen individuals' personalities, I have dedicated a significant amount of time in completing one narrative. Repeated meetings were held with the editor-in-chief of an international pharmaceutical periodical, and lady editor, to go over each and every word, phrase, until we were all satisfied with the text. This process was essential to ensure that reading the end result would be an enjoyable experience.

In an effort to provide readers with an understanding of myself, the author, with a fear of being overly presumptuous, allow me to introduce my lineage. To make a comparison with the renowned author, Soseki (Natsume), is highly impertinent, we

による将門追討祈願の寺）には行かない。世紀の改革者であった平清盛や信長（平氏）と同じで、端くれの私も、血が騒ぐ方である。しかし平素は実におとなしく、前著書の『素心』の「ぶれない・やさしい」が正直なところである。

私は、小林五左衛門の十代目である。現在の茨城県坂東市（旧・猿島郡飯島村）に来て約三百年に至っている。田畑となった開墾地は、戦後の農地改革により文無しになった。父（第九代目）・母ともに水戸の朱子学の影響下にあり、戦中は翼賛会の代表を務め公職追放となった。屋敷も二千坪あったが、庭の草取りと残った田畑を細々と耕していたのが父・母の姿である。子供（姉・妹と私）の教育には熱心であった。父が胃がんで亡くなる一週間前に見舞った時、私に言った言葉が「勉強をしろよ」だったのには返す言葉がなかった。私たち姉・僕・妹は、両親の愛情の下、仲が良かった。しょっちゅう喧嘩をしていたが。姉の落合絢子はがんで亡くなったが、兄貴（義理）は現在九十三歳で健在である。また、妹の藤代節子は、夫（和夫）をがんで亡くした。偶然ではあるが、姉と妹の連れ合いは東大法学部で同級生（旧制都立高校と旧制一高出身）であった。

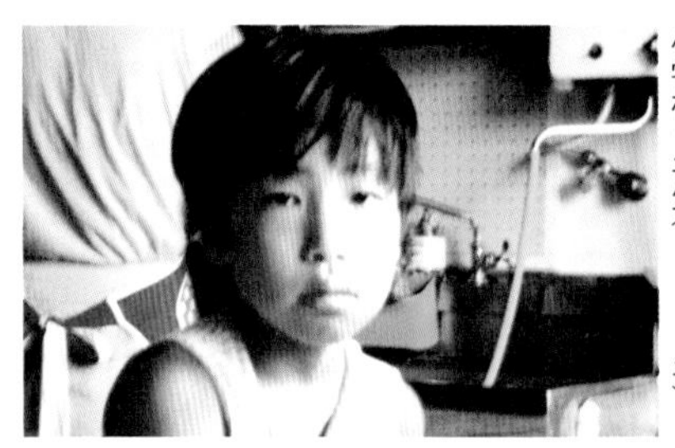
小学校6年生（1973年）

旧羽田空港での見送り

姉絢子（落合武雄、宏樹・伸夫（甥））

both hail from the same village leader. I come from an old established family. Comparing.

The sixth item of the Kyoho Reforms (1716–1737) introduced by the Eighth Shogun, Yoshimune Tokugawa, was a policy which emphasized the importance of agriculture, which lead to the swampland located between Mt. Tsukuba and Tone River cleared and cultivated to create farming fields by a believer of the Ikko Sect of Jyodo Shin Buddhism and a follower of Taira No Masakado, is the patriarch of a family lineage that continues to this day. This is why I do not go to Narita Shinsho Ji (temple) which was is known as a temple dedicated in the mid-Heian period to offer prayers in hunting down Masakado. Same as the great reformers of their century, such as; Taira No Kiyomori and Nobunaga (a Taira Clan descendent) although I may be on the

**上原家（父方）従弟会**

上原家ご母堂96歳の誕生日（2022年5月7日）

**川島家（母方）従弟会**

川島房宣氏

池田正純氏

池田八郎氏

川島安則氏

*Canberra Grandma Kay, and our children Yoko-Kazuhiko-Natsuko at kobayashi Garden*
キャンベラおばーちゃんと子供達、陽子（次女）、一彦（長男）、夏子（長女）小林家にて（1973）

長女夏子（大嶋尚志、宏一・美希（孫））

fringes, I believe I share the characteristic of getting excited. Although ordinarily very quiet, my book [Soshin-Unwavering・Kind] is actually realistic.

I am the tenth generation from my ancestor Isaemon Kobayashi. Arriving in the current Bando City, Ibaragi Prefecture (formerly known as Ijima Village, Sashima County) remaining for an estimated 300 years. Although owning the farming fields that was made through clearing the land, through the farming land reforms introduced after the war (World War II), it was made penniless. My father (ninth generation) as well as my mother, were students in the style of Cheng-Zhu schooling, from which influenced him to become a representative of the Yoku San Kai during the war, resulting in his expulsion from official employment. The residence was substantial, with 6,600m2, I have memories of the figure of my father and mother weeding the garden and minutely working the remaining farming fields. They were dedicated on the education of their children (my elder sister, myself and younger sister).

One week prior to his death by stomach cancer, I made a visit to see him, on that occasion his words to me were [make sure you study], to which I could not find the words in response. We siblings, my sisters and I, with love and affection from our parents, always got along. Although we often had our quarrels. I lost my elder sister, Ayako Ochiai to cancer, her husband, my elder brother-in-law is doing well at the age of 93 years old. Furthermore, my younger sister, Setsuko Fujishiro lost her husband,

キャンベラ・ホスピタル(1969)

送別会(1970)

今の私は、妻・順子も天に召されて、一人で暮らしているがすこぶる元気で毎日大学に通っている。海外にも年数回は一人旅をする。2019年には、アレキサンダー大王の足跡をたどるため、マケドニアに一週間一人旅をした。もちろん、マケドニア大学の国際関係論の院生を案内人に雇ったが、非常に親切であった。マケドニア人の98パーセントは、正統派キリスト教徒である。

亡妻・順子とは、三人の子供に恵まれた。小児科医になった一彦（長男）（十一代、妻／美千子・孫（芙実子・美菜子・麻衣子））。夏子（長女）（夫・大嶋尚史／半導体・孫（美希・宏一））。そして陽子（次女）である。この陽子は、交通事故で夭逝した。この陽子の事故は、家族にとって生涯解決のできない出来事となった。神が私に課した苦役・試練・贖罪と思い、常に親鸞の「唱えれば、神も仏も無かりけり、南無阿弥陀仏・南無阿弥陀仏と今も亡妻・順子と一緒に唱えている。また、子供たちや孫たちには、『国際人になるためのInsight Track』『素心――ぶれない・やさしい』、そして『敬人　つれづれに人（ひと）を敬う』を書いた十代目と思ってもらうとありがたい。でも、まあ一百歳までは生きたい・行きたい。

宏一（7歳）　美希（9歳）（2007）

Kazuo, to cancer. Although a complete coincidence, the spouses of both, older and younger sisters, were same year graduates of the University of Tokyo, Faculty of Law, (graduates of the old system municipal high school and old system Ichi high school).

Myself these days, with my wife Junko taken to heaven, although I live alone, I am extremely healthy and commute every day to the university. I travel abroad several times a year alone. Last year (2020), to follow the footsteps of Alexander the Great, I traveled alone to Macedonia for one week. Of course, I hired an international relations post-graduate student of the Macedonia University as a guide, he was extremely thoughtful and kind. Ninety-eight percent of the population of Macedonia are Orthodox Catholics.

My deceased wife, Junko and I were blessed with three children. My son, Kazuhiko, (eleventh generation, wife Michiko, and granddaughters (Fumiko, Minako, Maiko)), has become a pediatrician. My elder daughter Natsuko, (husband Hisashi Oshima/semiconductor, grandchildren (Miki and Koichi)), and my younger daughter, Yoko. This Yoko was taken far too early from us by a traffic accident. Yoko's accident was, for our family, was an event that would never be resolved. I have come to believe that this was God's imposition of labor, trial and punishment, resulting in my turn toward the Buddhist monk Shinran's [Through chanting, there is no longer a God or Buddha, Namu Ami Dabutsu] thus, I pray the words [Namu Ami Dabutsu] with my deceased wife Junko. In addition, I would be grateful if my children and grandchildren will remember the tenth generation who wrote [To Become an International Person Insight Track], [Soshin-Unwavering·Kind] and [Globalization – Respecting People I Pass the Time]. I hope to live to be a 100.

長男一彦は、キャンベラのプレスクールではよく動き回って友達も多く、誕生会にはよく招かれていた。人気者であった。帰国後、小児科医となり頑張っていて（妻:美千子/孫：芙実子・美菜子・麻衣子)、日本の少子化阻止に貢献している。

## 執筆者

# 小林 利彦（1936年〜）

自宅にて（1937年1月）

オーストラリア国立大学大学院「ジョーン・カーテン・メジカル・リサーチ・インステチュート」から
帰国後（1970年）、三菱油化（株）医薬事業部つくば医薬研究所の責任者として入社。
後、取締役。10数年を過ごし、その間多くの新薬の研究開発に貢献した。
当時、日本最初のバイオ製品となった組織培養ウロキナーゼの開発は、
米国アボット社との共同開発であった。
それが縁で、米国アップジョン社（ミシガン州カラマズー市）・米国 E.リリー社（インデアナ州、
インデアナポリス市）のR＆D研究所デビジョンVP（アジア・ジャパン担当副社長）として
勤めた（1986－2010年）。国内外を、飛び回っていた。
傍ら、文筆活動も盛んで著書（和文・英文併記）に、『国際人になるためのInsight Track』、
『素心——ぶれない・やさしい』、『敬人　つれづれに人（ひと）を敬う』がある。
そんな訳で、専門は「再生医療（幹細胞）と文筆家」と称している。
東大卒、オーストラリア国立大学医系大学院（博士）

## Author

# *Toshi(-Hiko) Kobayashi Ph.D.* *(1936~)*

**Specialized in Re-generative Medicine(Stem-Cell), and an author such as the three(3) books : Respecting People for Becoming Internationally, SOSHIN … Cool and Empathy, and Respecting People, As the Time Being Passed.**

**B.Sc.(U-Tokyo), Ph.D.(ANU)**

1942, April

Jun and Toshi (2009, May)

本籍地：〒306-0616 茨城県坂東市猫実新田526

# 敬人

**つれづれに人（ひと）を敬う　【和文・英文】**

2022年7月22日　第1版第1刷発行

著　　者　小林 利彦
発 行 者　林　諄
発 行 所　株式会社日本医療企画
〒104-0032　東京都中央区八丁堀3-20-5
S-GATE八丁堀
TEL 03-3553-2861（代表）
FAX 03-3553-2886
http://www.jmp.co.jp
印 刷 所　図書印刷株式会社

ISBN978-4-86729-126-9 C0036